World History

Pre-History to 1500 A.D. Reader and Workbook

Benjamin Kline
DeAnza College

KENDALL/HUNT PUBLISHING COMPANY
4050 Westmark Drive   Dubuque, Iowa 52002

Maps on pages 97 through 101 courtesy of www.theodora.com/maps. Used with permission.

Contents

Instructions:
Place the number of the blank
next to the proper term
on the bottom of the page

Humanity, Nature and Western Culture:
A Brief Historical Survey
Pre-History to c. 500 B.C
by
Benjamin Kline

When does humanity's ___[1] with nature begin to divurge from that of the rest of the animal kingdom? That is, when do it's actions no longer seem simply instinctual and instead are motivated by that unique awareness and/or intelligence that makes this species so unique. The connection between human action and technology seems to be the clearest answer to this question. When human awareness and intelligence enabled it to fashion _[2] for the more efficient exploitation of nature the true break with pure instinct began. This development begins during the ___[3], about two to three million years ago, when the earliest true humans (genus Homo) began to appear. Most of human evolution therefore occurred during the Pleistocene Epoch, which stretches from about 2.5 million years ago to the present. The Pleistocene has been a time of unusually great _

_____[4] variation when compared to most of the history of the Earth. Comparatively short warm periods have alternated with periods of _____[5], when the climate cooled and ice sheets spread from the poles.

---

glaciation	5
tools	2
relationship	1
Environmental	4
Pleistocene Era	3

The Paleolithic Period, or _____ [6], is the earliest and longest stage of human cultural development, lasting from about 2.5 million to about 10,000 years ago. The concept of a Paleolithic Period was proposed in 1865 by the English antiquarian _____ [7]. Like most of the archaeologists at the time, Lubbock had accepted the chronological validity and comprehensiveness of the three-age system first proposed (1836) in Denmark by C. J. Thomsen (1788-1865)--a scheme which stated that stone implements had preceded bronze tools, which in turn had preceded iron use in antiquity. Lubbock and his colleagues working elsewhere in Europe soon realized that the Stone Age itself should be divided into a later ___ [8] (New Stone Age), characterized by ground stone tools, and an earlier, much longer Paleolithic Period, newly recognized by them and represented by chipped _____ [9], sometimes associated with the bones of extinct species such as mammoth and cave bear. The transition between Lubbock's two periods was later termed the Mesolithic Period (Middle Stone Age). On the basis of observations made especially in France, the Paleolithic Period was divided by the late 19th century into three phases: the Lower, or Early, Paleolithic, characterized by the use of bifaces, or _ [10]; the Middle Paleolithic, when flake tools largely replaced bifaces; and the Upper, or Late, Paleolithic, distinguished by the use of blade tools. This scheme is still in use today in Old World Archaeology, although the scheme is evidently not valid for all areas nor does it imply necessarily that the passages from one phase to another took place simultaneously.

Paleoanthropologists now recognize three species of humans--Homo sapiens, or modern

---

hand axes	10
stone implements	9
Old Stone Age	6
Neolithic Period	8
Lubbock	7

humans, and the extinct __[11] and Homo Habilis. The three species share many traits, including an upright gait, sophisticated technological skills, engagement in cultural activities (such as communal hunting), and relatively large _____[12]. The genus _____[13] appears to have been confined to Africa, where it existed during the time range between 5.5 and 1 million years ago. Although primitive in some respects, Australopithecus is classified within the human family, _____

_____[14], because it shares with humans certain significant advances over earlier forms. In particular, its leg bones show that it walked upright; its brain, although still within the ape range, was relatively larger than that of most apes; and neither sex had the projecting canine teeth (fangs) that are used by apes in fighting. Presumably, Australopithecus used simple clubs or threw stones, instead of biting, to defend itself. Australopithecus varied considerably in size--from less than 1.2 m (4 ft) to about the size of a _____[15].

From deposits dating from about 2 million years ago have emerged the first direct evidence of behavior that decisively separates the species Homo from other animals. This behavior includes the regular use of stone tools and other artifacts and the life-style called hunting and gathering. In contrast to the foraging of nonhuman primates, the hunting and gathering of the first humans involved a division of labor. Some group members (probably males) hunted animals for meat, whereas the rest searched for small game and wild vegetable foods.

Australopithecus	13
modern human	15
Homo Erectus	11
Hominidae	14
brain cases	12

All shared the ___[16] they collected. This cooperative way of life strongly favored the evolution of technology (cutting tools and containers, especially). Additionally, there is evidence that these early humans meticulously planned their hunts. So the human capacity for abstract _____ _____[17], foresight, and adaptation to local conditions of life also apparently improved. The evidence for these changes is seen in the gradually increasing size of the brain, the development of increasingly complex technology (represented by stone working), and the rapid geographical spread of the human species.

After the extinction of Australopithecus, no more than one hominid species existed at any time. However, the single human species is given different names at different stages of its evolution. The earliest humans are known as _____[18]. Physically, they were much like Australopithecus, apart from the larger size of their brains. Most Homo habilis fossils have been discovered in East Africa. They are often found with simple _[19] tools, including stone choppers, cores, and sharp-edged flakes. At some sites evidence exists that animals up to _[20] size were butchered and eaten, but whether the meat was obtained by hunting or by scavenging the carcasses of dead animals has not been determined.

hippopotamus	20
Oldowan	19
Homo habilis	18
thought	17
food	16

As well as favoring the evolution of the brain, the early development of [21] and culture also affected the evolution of the teeth and jaws. As tools (and later fire) were used to prepare and soften food, the teeth of early humans became smaller and the jaws less robust. By about 1.6 million years ago, these trends had produced a mentally and physically more advanced population called __ [22]. At about the same time, the hand ax, a finely chipped, versatile, two-edged stone implement first appeared. Hand axes typify the _____ [23] tool industry, which also included a variety of pounders and flakes.

Although first recognized in Asia (Java man and Peking man), Homo erectus populations also lived throughout the warmer parts of the Old World. In Europe the jaw of Heidelberg man and many scattered hand axes attest to their presence (although some researchers consider this fossil to belong to an archaic Homo Sapiens). In _____ [24] both fossil remains and habitation sites have been found throughout the length of the continent, from Algeria to __ [25]. On the whole, Homo erectus seems to have preferred open or lightly wooded country, where game would have been most plentiful. Many sites attest to the skill of these people in hunting big game-- elephants, antelope, and even giant baboons--as well as gathering small game and vegetable foods. Although the colder regions of the far north were not inhabited, Homo erectus was sufficiently

Africa	24
Acheulean	23
Homo erectus	22
technology	21
South Africa	25

adaptable to survive in a variety of habitats, from tropical Africa to chilly central _____

_____ [26]. Undoubtedly, the more rigorous climate of the north stimulated technological

inventions. One of the most important of these was the use of _ [27], in cooking, for warmth, and in

the hunt. This vital step probably occurred about 500,000 years ago.

By about 250,000 years ago humans had become sufficiently advanced to be assigned to

Homo Sapiens. However, until about 40,000 years ago, they were not identical to modern humans.

They retained many ancestral features recalling Homo erectus: a large face with big teeth and a low

skull with heavy brow ridges and little or no forehead. In brain size, however, they were within the

modern range, which distinguishes them from the small-brained _____ [28].

An important sign of technological advance was the invention, about 100,000 years ago,

of the Levallois technique of stone working, in which a large thin flake is struck from a core and

used as a blank for making more specialized tools such as knives and scrapers. The makers of the

_____ [29] tools were the _____ [30] (Homo sapiens neanderthalensis), who flourished

between 100,000 and 40,000 years ago. Far from being the brutish, semierect "apemen" of

popular imagination, the Neanderthalers were an advanced human group whose ingenuity enabled

them to wrest a living from the most challenging habitat then occupied by humankind. 60,000

Neanderthanlers   30

Homo erectus   28

Mousterian   29

China   26

fire   27

years before present -- Earliest probable evidence of fire used deliberately to clear forests in the

_____ [31] Falls site in Tanzania.. Mousterian tools were adapted to a wide variety of tasks: cutting and preparing meat, scraping hides, working wood, and many others. Evidence of rituals--and careful burial of the dead--suggests the existence of _____ [32]. Some of the burials are of aged or handicapped people who must have been supported by the rest of the group, perhaps in return for the benefit of their wisdom and knowledge. Given the evidence for ritual and complex beliefs, it is likely that the brain of archaic Homo sapiens was sufficiently evolved to permit the use of true language. However, anthropologists are divided over whether the __ [33] were sufficiently developed to be capable of human speech. About 40,000 years ago humans of

_____ [34] type replaced the archaic humans such as the Neanderthalers.

In Europe and elsewhere in the ____ [35] the remains of the earliest physically modern humans occur with tools that attest to the invention of new techniques of manufacture, especially the production of long, narrow flake tools, called blades. These innovations define a new period of prehistory, the Upper Paleolithic. Hunting of animals and gathering of eggs, insects, and edible plants were the dominant economic activities. On the evidence of surviving hunting-gathering societies, it may be supposed that a dual economy existed in which men hunted and women gathered. By the end of the Paleolithic, humanity's technological repertoire included stone tools,

---

modern	34
Old World	35
Kalambo	31
religious beliefs	32
vocal chords	33

7

the use of fire, ___[36] and spear throwers, the bow and arrow, simple oil lamps, pigments, mortars and pestles, and bone sewing needles.

In the Old World this period began about 40,000 years ago, in the middle of the last glaciation. In the Americas the comparable stage, the _____[37], began at least 20,000 years ago with the migration of people across the Bering Strait from Siberia. In both continents culture based on _____[38] reached its peak of development during this period. Hunters became more expert, devising sophisticated techniques that involved large numbers of people working in cooperation to kill whole herds of game. In areas such as West and Central Europe, where game was most plentiful, permanent communities sprang up, and the population rose in numbers and density. Besides the stone _____[39], which could be fashioned into any one of a variety of handy small tools, technical innovations included tools made of bone and ivory, clothing sewn together and decorated with beads, and among some groups a system of reckoning time by the Sun and Moon. Among the finest productions of the [40] are the paintings and engravings (mostly animal representations) executed on stone slabs or ivory or on the walls of caves. The quality of this art is such that for many years critics refused to believe that it could be the work of prehistoric peoples. Even today, when its authenticity is established, its function is still obscure but is thought to have

---

spears	36
Upper Paleolithic	40
blade	39
hunting and gathering	38
Paleo-Indian	37

involved hunting magic or a _____ [41].

About 10,000 years ago the ice sheets and tundra vegetation in the north gave way rapidly to coniferous and hardwood forest. The great herds of _____ [42] ,horses, reindeer, and mammoths were replaced by more elusive, hard-to-hunt animals such as moose and elks. Human society and technology evolved in adaptation to the changing conditions. The resulting cultures are called _____ [43] in the Old World and Archaic in North America. New tools included microliths, tiny stone blades that were hafted in wood or antler handles. New weapons such as the bow and arrow enabled hunters to pursue the solitary game animals of the forest. Ingenious traps, snares, and nets enabled people to exploit resources such as wildfowl and fish that abounded in the lakes left by the retreating glaciers. Settlements became smaller, more dispersed, and less permanent. The _____ [44] transition is characterized by the origins of food production through the development of animal and plant husbandry. There is indirect evidence that the sheep was domesticated in the _____ [45] about 9000 B.C.. Over the next three millennia wild cereal plants were domesticated, animal and plant husbandry were further developed, and small farming communities were formed

Middle East	45
Mesolithic	43
bison	42
Neolithic	44
ritual use	41

(often in upland areas, where rainfall was adequate). _____ [46] was accomplished with the use of the digging stick and the wood hoe. The Paleolithic division of labor persisted into the Neolithic Period, with men tending herds of animals and women managing garden plots. Late Neolithic stone tools were improved by polishing, and polished stone axes were used to prepare forest clearings for cultivation. Modern tests with Neolithic axes have demonstrated their remarkable effectiveness in the felling of ___ [47]. Neolithic crafts included pottery, spinning and weaving, basketmaking, and house building. The discovery of Neolithic artifacts on islands in the Mediterranean also testified to the early use of boats

In some areas humans adapted in a markedly different way to the end of the glaciation. Rather than diversifying their use of resources, as the Mesolithic people of the northern woodlands were doing, they focused their attention on a few reliable resources. The Neolithic Period, or ____ _____ [48], refers to the stage of prehistoric cultural development that followed the Paleolithic and transitional Mesolithic periods and preceded the Bronze Age. In the 1920s the English archaeologist _____ [49] ascribed to the Neolithic four characteristic traits; these included, in addition to the grinding and polishing of ___ [50], the practice of agriculture, the domestication of animals, and the manufacture of pottery. The first and last of these criteria are no longer considered essential to a definition of the Neolithic. Archaeological research at the sites of Jarmo,

---

Cultivation	46
trees	47
New Stone Age	48
Miles Burkitt	49
stone tools	50

Jericho, and Shanidar in the _____ [51] has shown that the manufacture of pottery and polished-stone tools did not occur there until at least two millennia after the first appearance of ___

_____ [52] and animals.

Today agriculture and animal domestication are generally recognized as the hallmarks of Neolithic culture. The domestication of plants and animals provided prehistoric populations with a stable food supply, which in turn encouraged the establishment of permanent settlements resulting eventually in the rise of urban civilization. Although thousands of plant and animal species exist, only ___ [53] and about 50 animal species have been domesticated. About 12 or 13 plant crops are important staples, and almost all of these are grains--especially wheat, rice, and maize (corn)--that were domesticated from wild grasses by deliberate cultivation of their seeds. _____ [54] were the first animals to be tamed, usually to help in hunting. In the Near East such herd animals as goats, sheep, and cattle were domesticated. The _____ [55] that marked the beginning of agricultural civilization was the ox-drawn plow. It originated in the Middle East in the 4th millennium B.C.. Although the circumstances of its invention are unknown, the early scratch plow (or ard) was probably derived through modifications of the Neolithic adze and the hoe. Because

---

invention   55

Dogs   54

200 plant   53

Near East   51

plants   52

11

traction was supplied by oxen, the provinces of animal _____ [56] and plant cultivation were

merged, and the dual economy that had originated in the Paleolithic was now replaced by an

economy of field cultivation. Combined with the techniques of fallowing, _____ [57], and flood

control that date from the same period, plow agriculture was successfully established in the rain-

sparse river valleys of Mesopotamia, Egypt, and India, and the breakthrough to civilization was

accomplished. Plow agriculture was accompanied by an array of momentous developments.

Writing evolved; the political state came into being (possibly through the conflicting pressures of

expanding population and limited fertile land in the river valleys); _____ [58] set in; and copper and

bronze metallurgy was devised

Western Asia is the best-known, and perhaps the earliest, center of domestication, but

several other early centers existed in various parts of the world. In Mexico an agriculture was

developed on the basis of maize, __ [59], and squash. Other less-well-known centers of plant and

animal domestication existed in Southeast Asia, China, and probably tropical _____ [60]. In

areas adjacent to some of these centers food production spread as hunters were displaced by

farmers or acquired domesticates from their neighbors. The land to the east of the Mediterranean

was one such area with evidence of this new orientation. Some of the earliest examples of human

action and environmental decay come from this region and include:

'beans   59

'Africa   60

chronic warfare   58

'irrigation   57

'husbandry   56

7000 B.C. -- Emergence of Catal Huyuk, Jarmo and Alosh cultures in the Middle East and the destruction of lush forests may have given rise to myths about the __
61
.

6000 B.C. -- Deforestation leads to collapse of communities in southern Israel / Jordan.

Gradually, some populations began to concentrate on exploiting wild sheep and goats and a few species of wild grasses that produced edible seeds. The _____ ^{62} record reveals that a mutual dependence developed between the human populations and the animals and plants they exploited and protected. The favored species, breeding under human protection, became modified so that they could not have survived without it. The humans, in turn, living in permanent settlements near the resources they exploited and tended, could not easily revert to nomadic hunting. The people had become _____ ^{63}, and the animals and plants, domesticates.

In southwest Asia the cultivation of wheat and _____ ^{64}--the basic food cereals in the Western world--coupled with the domestication of food animals such as sheep, goats, pigs, and later cattle, first occurred in the period between _____ ^{65}. The earliest known sites containing evidence of Neolithic culture traits associated with sedentism, or early settled life, are found in the .

farmers	63
barley	64
Archaeological	62
9000 and 5000 B.C.	65
Garden of Eden	61

_____ [66] area of the Near East. Early remains have also been found in Greece, in Anatolia--notably at Catal Huyuk--and in Egypt. In the development of the Neolithic in Europe, the impulses toward early farming came mainly via the waterway routes from the Near East.

The earliest known evidence of food production in Europe dates from about 6500 B.C. at the Greek site of _____ [67]. Its Neolithic inhabitants cultivated wheat and barley before they knew pottery. The early spread of Neolithic cultures can be traced at a number of sites along the Danube River, such as Starcevo (c.5500 B.C.) and Lepenski Vir (c.5000 B.C.). By about 4000 B.C. cereal crops and cattle were introduced to western France and Switzerland, probably via the Mediterranean. Agriculture and domestic animal stock were in use in southern Scandinavia and in the northern European plains by about 3500 B.C., pushing the remaining _____ [68] peoples farther north into the wilderness or influencing them to adopt the new, settled mode of life. At the extreme northwest corner of Europe from about 3500 B.C. on, the British Isles were at the receiving end of the Neolithic culture traits of many _____ [69] arriving by sea and overland from the continent.

In eastern Asia archaeologists have traced an independent invention of ceramics and polished-stone use, with the development of a distinct form of agriculture based on _____ _____ [70] and other native plants. Most of the domesticated animals appear to have been brought ultimately from the West, although chickens, pigs, and dogs could have been local domesticates in

---

peoples _69_
Argissa-Maghula _67_
rice _70_
Fertile Crescent _66_
hunter-gatherer _68_

14

China. Farming appears to have been first developed along the _____[71] with the Yang-Shao

culture, dating from about 4000 B.C.. Farther south in Thailand archaeologists have found

evidence of ground-stone tools, pottery, and slate knives possibly used for rice harvesting dating

from perhaps as early as 6800 B.C., several thousand years before agriculture appeared in China.

At Non Nok Tha, a mound site in northern Thailand on the ___[72], evidence of sedentary farming

was found dating from the 4th millennium B.C.. In the New World animal domestication and

agriculture based on maize, beans, and _____[73] cultivation appeared by 2500 B.C.; the term

Neolithic is generally not used, however, in the context of New World archaeology

Contrary to a common notion, prehistoric villagers did not live more easily than hunters.

Villagers tended to eat a poorer diet, work harder, and suffer from more diseases. However, they

also tended to produce more offspring and thus built up a much denser population. Moreover,

_____[74] and herding often exhausted the soil in a few seasons, forcing the early farmers to

move on and wrest new territory from the hunters. So powerful was this process that within a few

thousand years most hunting and gathering peoples had been replaced by cultivators or herders in

all continents except _____[75].

Along with their tendency to expand, food-producing societies are distinguished from

---

Australia	75
primitive agriculture	74
squash	73
Yellow River	71
Mekong River	72

hunter-gatherer societies by their emphasis on _____ [76]. A hunter's principal assets are his

weapon kit and his acquired skills. A farmer, by contrast, owns wealth in the form of land, herds,

and the right to call on the labor of his friends and kinfolk. If he is lucky in these respects, or

skillful in their management, he can both _____ [77] wealth and use it to buy the labor of

others. By passing his wealth to his heirs, he can create a family of hereditary "notables" or

headmen. In this way a stratified society emerges. Unmistakable indications of social

stratification appeared within a few thousand years of the beginnings of agriculture. Within a few

centuries more the process had culminated, in a few favored centers, in the appearance of complex

societies in which specialist artisans and merchants plied their trades, a _____ [78] elite presided

over religious ceremonials, and a bureaucratic organization commanded the labor of the landless.

And so, with the appearance of _____ [79], ended two million years of human prehistory.

Ancient World 3500 - 500 B.C.

The Bronze Age is the stage of prehistoric cultural development when bronze, an alloy of

copper and tin, first came into regular use in the manufacture of tools, weapons, and other objects.

It marks the transition between the Neolithic Period, when _____ [80] and weapons were

predominant, and the succeeding Iron Age, when the large-scale use of various kinds of metals was

stone tools	80
civilization	79
accumulate	77
priestly	78
property	76

introduced. The term originated as part of the three-age system (Stone Age, _____ [81], and

Iron Age) introduced (1816) by Christian Thomsen, a Danish museum curator. The three-age

system, initially used purely for museum classification, was later validated in stratigraphy observed

through archaeological excavations, first in Denmark and then in other parts of Europe. The

Bronze Age occurred at different times in different parts of the world. In most areas, the

development of bronze technology was preceded by an intermediary period when _____

_____ [82] was used. This stage, sometimes called the _____ [83], did not occur in some areas,

including ancient China and prehistoric Britain, where the transition was made directly from stone

to bronze technology. In certain ancient cultures in Africa and elsewhere, stone was replaced

directly by iron technology, and the _____ [84] was bypassed completely. These and other

variations raise the issue of how prehistoric cultures changed: whether objects of material culture

were exchanged, were introduced through invasions or _____ [85], or were the result of the

independent occurrences of technological advances. Archaeologists believe that in the

development of bronze metallurgy all these are possibilities.

Ancient Near East

Metallurgy was first practiced in the ore-rich highlands of eastern Anatolia, more than

---

Bronze Age	81
Bronze Age	84
copper	82
Copper Age	83
migrations	85

17

10,000 years ago. Initially, during what is termed the _____ [86] ("copper-stone")

Period, metals such as copper were treated like stone and beaten into shape with stones. The

earliest known artifacts produced by the smelting of copper date from about 3800 B.C. at the site

of Tepe Yahya, Iran. The bronze produced there presumably resulted from an accidental blending

of copper with other metals, thus forming a new mixture with better properties than copper alone.

Early forms of the new ___ [87] were composed of copper combined with arsenic or antimony. From

about 3000 B.C., when bronze implements were in common use in the ancient Near East, copper

was combined with _____ [88], which produced a stronger bronze.

Bronze has many characteristics that make it more useful than copper. It is more durable

and casts better than copper. When dented or bent, it can be reworked back into shape, and bronze

cutting tools, such as axes or knives, can be easily resharpened. In the hands of _____ [89],

bronze tools revolutionized the arts of woodworking and stoneworking. Bronze also served as a

new medium of _ [90] expression, and from the beginning of the 3d millennium B.C., members of

---

alloy	87
Chalcolithic	86
tin ore	88
artisans	89
artistic	90

the Mesopotamian elite were buried with luxurious bronze objects. The Royal __91__, of about 2800 B.C., contained some of the richest bronze finds known.

The development of bronze technology is associated with the rise of the earliest great urban civilizations. The scarcity of tin in the _____92___prompted the budding civilizations of Mesopotamia and Sumer to search for raw materials in new lands and thereby may have indirectly stimulated their expansion into new territories. In addition to specialized labor for the operation of mining, smelting, and casting, a complex trade network was established, which necessitated an administrative hierarchy, storage systems, computation and writing, and other characteristics of urbanism. The Sumerian epic of _____93_, describes vast tracts of cedar forests in what is now southern Iraq. Gilgamesh defies the gods and cuts down the forest, and in return the gods say they will curse Sumeria with fire (or possibly drought). Reality reflected myth when some of the first laws protecting the remaining forests were decreed in Ur in 2700 B.C.. . Despite these efforts by 2600 B.C. large scale commercial timbering of .94 in Phoenicia (Lebanon) were needed for export to Egypt and Sumeria . Similar commercial timbering was taking place in Southern India. Still by 2100 B.C., soil erosion and salt buildup have devastated _____95. One Sumerian wrote that the "earth turned white." Civilization moved north to Babylonia and Assyria.

Cemetery at Ur   91
Gilgamesh   93
Near East   92
cedars   94
agriculture   95

Again, deforestation becomes a factor in the rise and subsequent fall of these _____[96].

Iron Age

The Iron Age marks the period of the development of technology, when the working of iron came into general use, replacing _____[97] as the basic material for implements and weapons. It is the last stage of the archaeological sequence known as the three-age system (Stone Age, Bronze Age, and ____[98]).

Although iron is a more common metal than copper or tin, the technique of iron smelting is more complicated than that with the other ores, requiring repeated hammering at red heat to expel slag impurities (primarily stone fragments) before wrought iron can be produced. Precisely when and where iron was first smelted remains unknown. It is possible that the process was discovered accidentally, when local sources of copper and tin with which to make bronze were becoming scarce. Occasional objects of smelted iron are known from as early as 3000 B.C. in the ancient _____[99] and predynastic Egypt, but these objects were inferior in hardness to comparable objects produced in bronze.

True iron metallurgy began among the _____[100] in eastern Anatolia at some time between 1900 and 1400 B.C.. The art of iron smelting was perfected by the time of the fall of the Hittite empire (c.1200 B.C.), and by 1000 B.C. iron objects and the knowledge of iron metallurgy had

---

Near East   99

Hittites   100

bronze   97

civilizations   96

Iron Age   98

20

spread throughout the Near East and the Mediterranean and _____ [101] into Europe. This development marked the end of the Near Eastern Bronze Age, although bronze working was still in use for various __ [102] or prestige objects.

After about 900 B.C. the widespread mass production of iron implements gave rise to large-scale folk migrations that extended widely over the continents of Asia and Europe. The beginning of the European Iron Age varied from place to place, depending upon available sources of raw materials. Outside of Greece, the earliest use of iron in Europe occurred about 800-750 B.C. in the late __ [103] cultures of central Europe and northern Italy. Following the Urnfield culture came the Hallstatt period (700-450 B.C.) of the European Iron Age. In about 500 B.C. the technique of forging iron tools and jewelry was introduced in Europe, a technique that remained virtually unchanged until the Middle Ages. The ____ [104] migration of about 450 B.C., commonly referred to as the La Tene phase of Celtic culture, marked the division between the Early and Late _____ [105] in Europe. The end of the prehistoric Iron Age was heralded by the Roman expansion in the Alpine area as far as the Danube River (c.15 B.C.).

Celtic	103
westward	104
Urnfield	101
ritual	102
Iron Age	105

Early Agriculture in the Old World

The evolution from nomadic _____ [106] to cultivators allowed people to establish permanent villages because they had a reliable food supply close at hand. More people were freed from providing food and were able to develop technologies and services that led to the shift from farming communities to __ [107]; eventually, agriculture-based civilizations were formed.

In Mesopotamia, the region between the Tigris and Euphrates rivers in present-day Iraq, cultivation began in the 9th millennium B.C.. The wheel was invented, pulleys were used to draw water from artificial canals, and complex irrigation systems were constructed. _____ [108] raised wheat and other cereal grains; were skilled in gardening; and domesticated the camel, donkey, and horse.

Relying on the water and fertile silt of the Nile, Egyptians irrigated land to ensure large crops of wheat and barley, which, along with flax, provided the basis for their agriculture. Several types of _ [109] were cultivated, and wild papyrus was harvested to make paper. In addition to oxen and horses, the Egyptians kept poultry, sheep, goats, swine, and cattle.

The _____ [110] civilization of northern India, which existed from about 2300 to 1750 B.C., raised wheat, barley, and rice. These people grew such plants as cotton, sesame, tea, and sugarcane. Chickens were domesticated from Indian jungle fowl, and the water buffalo and

---

Hunter-Gatherers	106
Indus	110
palm trees	109
Mesopotamians	108
towns	107

22

zebu cattle were used as _¹¹¹ animals. Farmers used plows, designed effective _¹¹² systems, and

built large granaries. In urban areas, such as the Mohenjo Darro civilization of Indus River valley,

however there were high levels of public health and citywide sanitation. The Indus civilization

appears to have declined rapidly in the early 2d millennium B.C.. The archaeological evidence

indicates that the efficient urban administration of Mohenjo-daro had deteriorated by c.1750 B.C.,

when the construction of _¹¹³ markedly declined. Evidence has also been discovered of

intermittent and devastating floods from this time, and, intriguingly, the remains of 38 corpses

were found apparently left unburied in lanes and houses of the latest level of occupation. Some

scholars have postulated a final massacre, possibly by conquering _____¹¹⁴ peoples whose epics

refer to their conquest of walled cities. Others have attributed the decline to an _____¹¹⁵

catastrophe that created violent and recurrent flooding along the southern course of the Indus. Still

others suggest that the Indus civilization may have overextended itself, resulting in its collapse

under the combined onslaught of natural disasters and barbarian incursions.

Aryan	114
ecological	115
houses	113
draft	111
irrigation	112

Instructions:
Place the number of the blank
next to the proper term
on the bottom of the page

Humanity, Nature and Western Culture:
A Brief Historical Survey
Classical Age to Renaissance A.D.

Ancient Greece

By the 5th century B.C. two Greek city-states, Athens and _____ [1], dominated their

smaller and less wealthy neighbors. Sparta had gradually become the most powerful state on the

_____ [2] by conquering neighboring peoples. Its citizens lived a rigidly disciplined life. A

public assembly gave adult male citizens a slight voice in government, but a council of magistrates

(the Ephors) retained most powers, and Sparta's two kings provided military leadership.

Agricultural and military interests dominated Sparta. Athens was a much more diverse society,

with farmers, artisans, merchants, seafarers and other groups enjoying a sense of freedom that was

lacking in Sparta. Like Sparta, however, _____ [3] had a large slave population. By the 5th

century B.C. the majority of the male citizens had succeeded in taking control of the city's

government, which they called democracy, meaning "rule by the people." Many public positions

were filled by a _____ [4], and most Athenian citizens served at least once on the city's

governing council. The free exchange of ideas necessary to make this system work also

encouraged poetry, art, and philosophy. In the 5th and 4th centuries B.C. the religious festivals of

Athens brought forth notable _____ [5] by the playwrights Aeschylus,

Athens	3
Peloponnesus	2
Sparta	1
dramas	5
lottery	4

25

Aristophanes, _____ [6], and Sophocles. One of the greatest figures in Athens was the philosopher Socrates, whose ideas and manner of teaching were recorded by his student and disciple Plato. _____ [7], who held that the most important human activity is the search for truth, was accused of impiety, or teaching disrespect for the gods of Athens, and condemned to death in 399 B.C..

The free intellectual climate in which Athenian democracy flourished had helped bring philosophy and drama into being, but the trial of Socrates showed that rule by the majority could be abused. _____ [8], saddened by the death of his teacher, concluded that only a government by the wise could be just. One of Plato's students, __ [9], summarized the arguments for each of the forms of government represented in the Greek city-states. Aristotle warned that only a mixed government could provide a guarantee against either the tyranny of one or the tyranny of many. Arguments over politics were not confined to philosophers, however. The rivalry between Athens and Sparta, although put aside twice to defend Greece against Persian invasions, led to the _____ [10] War (431-404 B.C.) and to Athens's downfall.

The ancient Greeks were aware of the environmental problems their society had created and faced if not the solutions to the problems. By the 5th century the Greek coastal cities had

---

Socrates	7
Euripides	6
Plato	8
Aristotle	9
Peloponnesian	10

become landlocked after deforestation, which caused soil ____ [11]. The resulting siltation filled in the bays and mouths of rivers. Plato (427 – 347 B.C.) compared the hills and mountains of Greece to the bones of a wasted body: "All the richer and softer parts have fallen away and the mere skelton of the land remains." He adviced, "Since the land is the parent, let the citizens take care of her more carefully than __ [12] do their mother." One river located in Southwestern Greece, the Maender, became so silted that its twists and turns came to represent a river wandering – or _____

_____ [13]. The Greek physician _ [14] (460-377 B.C.), considered the father of medicine, noted the effect of food, of occupation, and especially of climate in causing disease. One of his books, *De aëre, aquis et locis* (*Air, Waters and Places*), is the earliest work on human ecology. The Greek general _____ [15], one of the first historians, wrote the history of Peleponesian War largely because his own mission to protect valuable timber lands in northern Greece failed.

The Roman Republic

To the west another people, similar to the Greeks in origin and institutions, was shaping an empire that was to be more durable. Founded, according to tradition, in the 8th century B.C., Rome had abolished (c.510 B.C.) its monarchy, which succeeded that of the Etruscans. As in Athens, the wealthy families (known in Rome as the patricians) who ruled the early city slowly gave way to pressures from the majority, which had originally been excluded from the government.

---

erosion	11
Thucydides	15
children	12
meandering	13
Hippocrates	14

In the _____ [16] the basic political institution was the Roman Senate, in which only the _____ [17] could serve. The plebeians, or commoners, gathered in a popular assembly, but they eventually exerted their greatest influence through the election of officials called Tribunes who could veto the acts of the Senate. Disputes between _____ [18] and patricians led to an agreement (c.450-449 B.C.) by which the city's laws were posted on 12 tablets for public inspection. This solution helped create a tradition of solving public problems through law.

In the 5th century B.C. Rome was no more than a city perched on the seven hills overlooking the _____ [19]; two centuries later Roman armies had conquered the neighboring Latins as well as the Greeks who had settled in the southern part of the Italian peninsula. By offering citizenship or privileged treatment to those peoples who would cooperate with them, the Romans were able to unify the entire peninsula by 270 B.C. and create a state that extended far beyond the city walls. Rome's expansion continued in wars with the north African city of _____ [20] and with Macedonia. By 30 B.C., Roman rule extended into Spain and parts of north Africa, including Egypt.

Tiber River	19
Carthage	20
patricians	17
plebeians	18
republic	16

Roman _____[21] made it possible to unify the varied peoples conquered by the Roman

armies. Roman jurists taught that above local customs and laws was a natural or universal law.

Cicereo(106-43 B.C.), the most eminent of these legal philosophers, identified __[22]with the ideal

truths proclaimed by Socrates and Plato and claimed that it could be understood by all reasonable

human beings and applied to all peoples. Thanks to this theory Roman administrators could feel

justified in overruling local customs and in imposing their own laws. Like its laws, Rome's

political institutions also evolved over the years. The expansion of Roman territory sharpened

internal conflicts, and after a prolonged civil war the general __[23]took command. His rise to power

marked an end to the political power of the Senate and the Roman citizen and doomed the

_____[24] form of government, which had become increasingly aristocratic. Caesar's enemies

assassinated him in _____[25]. Although Caesar himself had refused the title of emperor,

his successors, beginning with Augustus and Tiberius, ruled for life and passed their authority on

to their heirs. For all its violence and turmoil, the century of transition from the republic to the

empire (c.70 B.C.-c. AD 70) witnessed great creative achievements by Roman writers employing

the Latin language. The poet Vergil attempted to emulate the Greek epics with his Aeneid, and

Horace and Ovid brought deft wit to their poetry. The historians Livy and Tacitus and the

republican	24
law	21
Natural law	22
44 B.C.	25
Julius Caesar	23

philosopher Seneca carried on Cicero's tradition of combining scholarship with an active public career.

The Roman Empire

At its height, in the _____ [26], the Roman Empire extended from Britain and northern Europe along the Danube into Anatolia and as far as the rivers of Mesopotamia. It included more people and territory than any previous empire. The empire centered on the _____ [27], however; the most populous areas were close to the sea, which was also the principal highway. In ____ [28] and Anatolia Roman control was less secure beyond the narrow belt of settlements clinging to the sea, and nomads pressed on the empire's outer edges. Beginning in the 3d century AD, Germanic peoples increased their pressure on the western and northern parts of the empire. Some Germanic tribes were admitted to the _____ [29] districts of the empire as buffers against more violent tribes beyond. In addition, various Germanic tribes were recruited for service in the Roman army, but their service masked the fact that they had not completely absorbed Roman culture and _____ [30]. Increasingly, this subtly altered army intervened in the selection of emperors. Meanwhile, successive waves of barbarian tribes attacked the empire in force. The decline and fall of the Roman Empire clearly had an environmental dimension. The Romans placed too great a

---

frontier   29

2d century AD   26

Africa   28

Mediterranean   27

laws   30

demand upon the available _____ [31] and the result was that ecological failures interacted with social, political, and economic forces to assure that the vast entitiy called the Roman Empire would disappear or be changed beyond recognition. As residents of what had become the largest city in the world, ancient Romans were well aware of the problem of air pollution.   They called it _____ [32] (heavy heaven) or infamis aer (infamous air). Odors and runoff from_____ [33], sewage and industries such as smelting or tanning also fouled the air and water. The Roman poet _____ [34] and many of his contemporaries criticized "The smoke, the wealth, the noise of Rome..." By 100 AD occupational diseases were well known in ancient Rome. Workers in lead and mercury mines and smelters were known to suffer from the metals, according to Rome's famous engineer Vitruvius. While slaves were often used in the lead and mercury mines, Plutarch recommended that only criminal slaves be used. It was not just, he said, to expose non-criminals to these conditions.   Pliny the Elder noted the use of bladders as respirators by workers in zinc smelters.

As dirty as Rome must have been, the Romans are also remembered for setting a new standard for public health. Public physicians were appointed to attend the poor, and hospitals were built throughout the empire. The city of Rome had _____ [35] bringing clean water to gymnasiums and public baths. Many areas of the city had sewage or used reservoirs for sending freshets of waters to sweep streets clean. A similar level of public health would not return to

---

aquaducts	35
natural resources	31
garbage	33
gravioris caeli	32
Horace	34

Europe until the mid 18th century or later. Efforts to combat the affects of _____ [36] can

be seen throughout Roman history. By 500 B.C. Cloaca Maxima (big sewer) was built in Rome

by the Etruscan dynasty of Tarquins. As Rome grew, a network of cloacae (sewers) and aquaducts

were built. In 80 A.D. the _____ [37] passed a law to protect water stored during dry periods so it

could be released for street and sewer cleaning. In 100 AD experiments with solar powered pumps

were taking place in Rome. Despite such efforts the decline of the Roman Empire may have been

partly due to pollutants, particularly lead poisoning.

Roman and Early Medieval Agricultural Innovations

The flowering of agricultural civilization in Europe north of Rome during the Middle

Ages was foreshadowed by Roman technical innovations. Roman engineers were familiar with the

principle of the _____ [38] and its associated gearing as early as the 1st century B.C., and they

occasionally employed it in the construction of mills. Even more important was the development

of a heavy plow capable of turning the _____ [39] of northern Europe. The ancient light

_____ [40] drawn by a pair of oxen was effective in the dry climates of the Middle East and the

Mediterranean world, where the soils were light and friable. In northern Italy and in transalpine

Europe the light plow permitted tillage only on well-drained upland soils, whereas the wet,

clay soils	39
water wheel	38
Roman Senate	37
pollution	36
plow	40

cohesive soils of the vast lowlands and the north European plain could not be _____ [41]. The

heavy plow with its vertical _____ [42], horizontal plowshare, and moldboard to turn the soil,

mounted on wheels and drawn by teams of four, six, or eight animals yoked in pairs, made possible

the civilization of northern Europe. During Roman times a coulter was sometimes used, and the

light plow was occasionally mounted on wheels; development was slow, however, and it was only

in the 9th and 10th centuries that the fully developed heavy plow came widely into use and began

to transform ____ [43]. The depth of the cut made by the heavy plow and the overturning of the sod

allowed extensive tracts of fertile land to be opened to cultivation.

The Romans advanced farm technology in the Mediterranean world by making tools,

including the plow, reaper, hoe, and sickle, that had iron parts. They cultivated wheat, barley, and

_____ [44], kept vineyards, and raised livestock. Before 200 B.C., Roman farmers were

independent, each owning about 1.8 to 6.1 ha (4 to 15 acres). During the next 200 years the

wealthy acquired publicly owned lands until they each controlled hundreds or thousands of _____

_____ [45], which were worked by slaves. Throughout this period a series of agrarian laws were

enacted to divide land held by the wealthy and distribute it to small farmers. These attempts at

land reform eventually failed, and by AD 200 many farmers were tenants on estates. By AD 400

---

millet   44
hectares   45
Europe   43
coulter   42
cultivated   41

the rights of these tenants were reduced until they became _____ [46], bound to the land.

Biblical Justification for Dominating Nature

In 1967, the historian _____ [47]., published a short essay in *Science* called "The Historical Roots of Our Ecological Crisis." White contended in this essay that Western society's relationship with nature is based principally on the exploitative philosophy of its Judeo-Christian tradition. Several scholars and theologians sharply challenged White's argument. The scholar Rene Dubos was particularly critical, maintaining that the people of pre-Christian Egypt, Mesopotamia, and Persia had equaled Western society's capacity for exploiting and damaging its _____ [48]. While it is true that many non-Western societies abused their environments to various degrees, White's argument provides some explanation for the West's energetic _____ [49] of nature and for its technological developments as well.

Christianity inherited from _____ [50] a faith in the continual progress of humanity. Change, the core of this belief, is considered part of the existing order of nature. Altering the environment is a key to this relationship, and change is an expected result of human

---

Serf   46

environment   48

Lynn White, Jr   47

exploitation   49

Judaism   50

development. We measure time as depicted in the book of _____ [51] in the Bible, where God took six days to bring his creation into existence. God first created light and darkness, and then the heavenly bodies, the planets, and all the other life forms except man. Finally, _____ [52] was created in God's image and given Eve to keep him company. Their position in this new world was made clear when God commanded.

> be _____ [53], and multiply, and replenish the earth, and subdue it: And have dominion over the fish of the sea, and over the fowl of the air, and over every living thing that moveth upon the earth.

Adam and Eve named all the animals, establishing their dominance over them. Although they were a special creation, Adam and Eve remained harmonious with nature, and peace and abundance pervaded the Garden of _____ [54]. However, after Adam and Eve ate the "forbidden fruit" of self-knowledge, they were cast out of Eden. As punishment, they were no longer in harmony with nature.

> …now, through thy act, the ground is under a curse. All of the days of thy life thou shalt win food from it with _____ [55]; thorns and thistles it shall yield thee, this ground from which thou dost win thy food. Still thou shalt earn thy bread with the sweat of thy brow, until thou goest back into the ground from which thou wast taken; dust thou art, and unto dust shalt thou return.

Eden	54
Genesis	51
toil	55
Adam	52
fruitful	53

Adam and Eve's actions destroyed the peace of _____[56]. The lamb no longer sat peacefully with

the lion. Even after Noah saved the creatures of the earth during the _____[57], humanity and

nature did not find a bond of understanding. God commanded Noah,

> All the beasts of earth, and the winged things of the sky, and the creeping things of earth, are
> to go in fear and dread of you, and I give you dominion over all the fishes of the sea. This
> creation that lives and moves is to provide _____[58] for you.

The word *dominion* is significant in this passage. Humanity might have been punished for its

misbehavior, but it nevertheless remained the dominant species on earth. Western society

embraced this concept of humanity's _____[59] over nature.

By the fifth century, Christianity had spread throughout the Roman Empire and was the

predominant faith. By the sixth century, most Western Europeans had converted to Christianity

from_____[60]. A nature-based religion, paganism taught that people and the natural world

were spiritually connected, were dependent on each other, and had a common bond. Pagans

believed spirits inhabited all of nature and were accessible to humanity. Spirits took many forms:

trees, rivers, mountains, fairies, centaurs, elves, and so forth. Out of respect, humans placated each

---

paganism	60
superiority	59
'Great Flood	57
food	58
'Eden	56

spirit before taking an _____ [61] to it, damming it, or mining it for ore. Christianity, by contrast, commanded people to exploit nature in their ongoing struggle for sustenance and life. Because both Adam and _____ [62] had been commanded to dominate nature, Christians felt justified in their efforts to harness nature.

Throughout the Middle Ages, ca. 500–1500, humans applied innovation and technology to overcome natural obstacles and to tame nature. In the more populated areas of the Mediterranean basin, where the soil was semi-arid, farmers used crude plows to scratch the earth into small, _____ [63] fields. By the seventh century northern farmers developed a new plow with a vertical knife, horizontal share, and mold-board that cut deeply into the often wet and solid soil. This innovative plow, found nowhere else in the world, provided a tool to help people assert their dominance over nature. That humanity was _ [64] the struggle over nature is evident in the way many artisans began to depict this relationship. As Lynn White, Jr., describes it,

The same exploitive attitude appears slightly before 830 a.d. in western illustrated calendars. In older calendars the months were shown as passive personifications. The new ____ [65] calendars, which set the style for the Middle Ages, are very different: they show man

winning	64
Frankish	65
Noah	62
squarish	63
ax	61

37

coercing the world around them—plowing, harvesting, chopping trees, butchering pigs. _____[66] and nature are two things, and man is master.

A quick succession of technological inventions followed, as Western Europeans strove to use and exploit their natural surroundings. Faced with constant and unrelenting force _____[67] succumbed to humanity's needs. Early industries, such as grain mills, used water power by the eleventh century and wind power by the late twelfth century. Labor-saving devices, including new _____[68], shoulder collars, wheeled plows, and power trains with cranks, appeared at a remarkable pace. Agricultural production increased as improved methods of tillage and animal husbandry were combined with new seed types and animal breeds. With the ability to cultivate more land and produce higher yields, the population of Western Europe rose from __[69] people between 700 and 1300.

By the fourteenth century the surpluses generated by agricultural expansion required entrepreneurial skills, managerial ability, and technological skills and inventiveness, which in turn stimulated trade and industry. Technologically, Western European society had become a global leader. The ill affects of this technological revolution were soon being felt. In 1157 the unendurable air pollution from wood smoke led Henry II's wife _____[70] of Aquataine to flee Tutbury Castle and 100 years later a similar occurence plaqued Queen Eleanor of Provence who

27 to 73 million	69
nature	67
harnesses	68
Man	66
Eleanor	70

was forced to leave Nottingham Castle for Tutbury Castle because heavy _____ [71] fouls

the air. By _____ [72] the British were already beginning to use and burn coal, calling them

"sea coals", because they were brought by barge or boat to London from Newcastle and other parts

of northeastern England. The air pollution created by the burning of this fuel caused ____ [73] in

1306 to forbid coal burning in London when Parliament was in session. Like many attempts to

regulate coal burning, it has little effect. Pollution and poor hygiene contributed to the devestating

affects of the Bubonic plague which hit Europe from th 1340s through the 1350s. Efforts were

quickly made to create the first attempts to enforce public health and quarantine laws. For

example, In 1366 the City of _____ [74] forced butchers to dispose of animal wastes outside

the city; similar laws would be disputed in Philadelphia and New York nearly 400 years later. In

1388 the British Parliament passed an act forbidding the throwing of filth and garbage into ditches,

rivers and waters. The City of Cambridge also passed the first urban _____ [75] laws in

England. Reaction to the plague also included genocidal pogroms against Jews in most cities of

Europe. One not very satisfying idea about this is that Jews, with greater understanding of

---

Paris	74
1300	72
sanitary	75
Edward I	73
coal smoke	71

elementary hygiene, may have had a lower infection rate, which in turn might have seemed

suspicious. People had no explanation for the _____ [76] other than rumor, superstition and vague

theories about miasmas and air pollution. It is estimated that _____ [77] population, over 25

million people, died of the plaqued during this period.

---

struggle   76

Crusades   77

A Survey of Ancient Asian History

In eastern Asia archaeologists have traced an independent invention of ceramics and polished-stone use, with the development of a distinct form of agriculture based on rice and other native plants. Most of the domesticated animals appear to have been brought ultimately from the West, although chickens, pigs, and dogs could have been local domesticates in China. Farming appears to have been first developed along the Yellow River with the Yang-Shao culture, dating from about 4000 BC. Farther south in Thailand archaeologists have found evidence of ground-stone tools, pottery, and slate knives possibly used for rice harvesting dating from perhaps as early as 6800 BC, several thousand years before agriculture appeared in China. At Non Nok Tha, a mound site in northern Thailand on the Mekong River, evidence of sedentary farming was found dating from the 4th millennium BC. In the New World animal domestication and agriculture based on maize, beans, and squash cultivation appeared by 2500 BC; the term Neolithic is generally not used, however, in the context of New World archaeology

In Asia, the Bronze Age of the Indus civilization began about 2500 BC. The Indus civilization of northern India, which existed from about 2500 to 1750 BC, raised wheat, barley, and rice. These people grew such plants as cotton, sesame, tea, and sugarcane. Chickens were domesticated from Indian jungle fowl, and the water buffalo and zebu cattle were used as draft animals. Farmers used plows, designed effective irrigation systems, and built large granaries. In urban areas, such as the Mohenjo Darro civilization of Indus River valley, however there were high levels of public health and citywide sanitation. The Indus civilization appears to have declined rapidly in the early 2d millennium BC. The archaeological evidence indicates that the efficient urban administration of Mohenjo-daro had deteriorated by c.1750 BC, when the construction of houses markedly declined. Evidence has also been discovered of intermittent and devastating floods from this time, and, intriguingly, the remains of 38 corpses were found apparently left unburied in lanes and houses of the latest level of occupation.

Some scholars have postulated a final massacre, possibly by conquering Aryan peoples whose epics refer to their conquest of walled cities. Others have attributed the decline to an ecological catastrophe that created violent and recurrent flooding along the southern course of the Indus. Still others suggest that the Indus civilization may have overextended itself, resulting in its collapse under the combined onslaught of natural disasters and barbarian incursions

China

Among the river valleys of China, people learned how to cultivate soybeans, oranges, peaches, pears, hemp, and tea. They kept livestock, practiced intensive gardening, and excelled at flower horticulture. The Yangshao is now firmly established as the earliest culture of the Hwang He Neolithic, starting before 5000 BC. The Longshan is now known to have been concentrated along the Pacific coast of China, from Shandong to Taiwan. In several locations, Longshan artifacts have been dated as early as those of the Yangshao. Thus, the derivation of the Longshan from the Yangshao, as some had proposed, is now a subject of some debate. Both the Yangshao and the Longshan were cultures of farmers, herdsmen, and hunters. Although the Yangshao planted millet in the plains of the cool and temperate Hwang He valley, the Longshan were the world's earliest known rice farmers in the milder and more humid coastal region. The last Neolithic culture of North China was the direct ancestor of the Shang dynasty (1600-c.1027 BC), which in part also drew upon the Neolithic cultures of western and eastern China. Known from several sites, most importantly Anyang and Zhengzhou, the emergence of the Shang civilization marked the first appearance of writing, bronze metallurgy, monumental architecture, and a genuinely urban way of life in China. In China, the use of bronze was introduced relatively late, probably during the early phases of the Shang dynasty (c.1600-1027 BC).

Ancient religions of Asia

In Asia are certain clearly recognized types of spiritual experience that occur in the West only incidentally and with a minimum of recognition by the official religious traditions. These types of experience should not always be identified with mysticism, or the sense of union with God, which may occur often in a theistic and religious context. It therefore seems best to use the term "ways of liberation" to describe these forms of spiritual experience, for all are concerned with liberating human consciousness from ideas and feelings brought about by social conditioning, that is, by the very systems of convention that a religion, in the usual sense of the term, guarantees. These ways should not be considered antireligious, however, for they seek not so much to destroy religion and convention as to use them without being bound by them. They endeavor to go beyond the view of the world acquired through the use of thought and language; they consider that this view overemphasizes the divisions and differences of things and tends to make people neglect their inseparability from the total universe.

Hinduism.

Historical Background

Scholars sometimes distinguish Vedism, the religion of ancient India based on the Vedas, from Hinduism, although it is difficult to pinpoint a time that demarcates them. The Vedas were hymns of the Aryans, who invaded in the 2d millennium BC.

Vedism stressed hope for a future existence in heaven and lacked the concepts of karma and rebirth; Hinduism characteristically includes karma and rebirth, and the greatest hope is for eventual release from their sway. The Vedic deities were somewhat different from those which dominate in Hinduism, although scholars have traced the origins of Vishnu and Shiva back to Vedic counterparts. Later Vedism is sometimes called Brahmanism because of the authority accorded the Brahmins, or priests, who performed the ritual Vedic sacrifice. However, the challenge of non-Vedic religions, notably Buddhism and Jainism, led to the replacement of the rigid Brahmanical rules by more relaxed and varied forms of worship. Although the Vedas continue to be spoken of as the final authority in Hinduism, other texts of equal importance exist. Thus, a literature was developed for each of the four aims of life: various Dharmasastras, such as the Code of Manu, which detail the duties of class and station; Kamasastras, such as the Kamasutras of Vatsyayana, handbooks of pleasure, erotic and otherwise; the Arthasastra, attributed to Kautilya (300 BC), which offers advice to a ruler as to how to keep the throne; and the philosophical literature of the various systems, which deals with liberation and how to achieve it.

In addition, certain collections of tales came to be widely known in popular life, especially the two great epics, the MahabaraaA and the Ramayana. The Mahabharata tells of five princes who were cheated out of their kingdom and who, after a period of banishment in the forest, returned to fight a victorious and righteous war to regain it. An especially beloved portion of this epic is the section called the Bhagavad Gita, in which Arjuna, one of the brothers, is counseled by his charioteer Krishna, an incarnation of Lord Vishnu. The Ramayana tells the story of the ideal Hindu man, Rama, whose wife Sita is abducted by a demon, and of Rama's journey to Sri Lanka to recapture her. Both epics are filled with didactic tales, edifying poems, and fables. It is probably through their constant retelling in the village that Hinduism is most efficiently disseminated from generation to generation. Another source of Hindu lore is the Puranas, collections of legends and myths.

The period from roughly 500 BC to AD 1000 is sometimes spoken of as that of classical Hinduism. It was during this period that the major literature was composed, the great philosophical systems developed, and the basic Vaishnava and Shaiva sects organized. After 1000, beginning in south India somewhat earlier, a spirit of devotional fervor coupled with social reform swept through India, and the period from that time until near the present is known as the bhakti period. During this time the forms of religious worship changed and diversified further. Singing of devotional songs and poems in the vernacular rather than in Sanskrit, the language in which practically all classical Hindu literature was written, is one example. Direct approach to the god was emphasized, and the mediating role of the priest somewhat curtailed. Love, a sentiment common to all but particularly to the most ordinary villager, is now celebrated as the way to the highest end; some bhakti philosophies hold that liberation is not the supreme goal and that loving service to God is a higher one.

Recent developments in Hinduism are indicative of a movement away from certain aspects of classical practice, such as SUTTEE, a widow's suicide at her husband's funeral; caste distinctions; and even karma and rebirth

Basic Beliefs

Within the cultural complex of Hinduism, which may be considered panentheistic, are a number of equally legitimate *darshana*, or points of view, which the individual may adopt. The most notable are Vedanta, based on the teachings of the , a body of poetic scriptures; and Yoga, a way of meditation believed indigenous to India. Both Vedanta and Yoga are concerned with liberation from the world, which is considered an illusion of reality.

Ordinarily, neither Vedanta nor Yoga is studied until a man has reached the middle of life, has established himself in his caste, which may be considered his role or vocation, and is ready to transmit his social duties to his sons. Thus, Vedanta and Yoga usually are not taught to children, as are the Scriptures and beliefs of such a religion as Christianity, but only to mature adults fully disciplined in the ways of society. These ways involve precisely giving up one's role and person and leaving the task of maintaining one's social obligations in order to prepare for death. The reason is that death is held to be a calamity when it comes to a person who still believes that he or she is a separate individual.

According to Vedanta, the idea that the world is a multiplicity of distinct things is considered *maya*, or an illusion, resulting from the conventional way of thinking. Because *maya* has the original meaning of "to measure," the world is thought to be measured or marked out by those divisions and classifications of human experience that words and ideas make possible. To describe a complicated curve, one must measure it as if it were a series of distinct points. Similarly, to describe and think about nature, one must break it up into manageable units or terms, that is, things and events. This procedure, however useful, gives the strong impression that events are separable from one another, that one could happen without another, and that pleasure could exist without

45

pain or life without death. A similar impression prevails concerning the separability of things.

Vedanta maintains that all distinctions are relative to each other and that opposites such as the knower and the known, the subject and the object, are distinctions as inseparable as the two faces of a coin. In other words, the world can be separated into independent things only in thought. In concrete fact the world is an inseparable unity or, more exactly, a nonduality, for unity is also a thought or idea existing only in relation to the idea of diversity. The true state of the world is neither unity nor multiplicity. The state of the world is rather immeasurable, indescribable, and indefinable.

A man may therefore recognize that in his deepest consciousness (*Atman*, in Hinduism) he is not this separate individual but , or the indefinable totality. He has been led, however, to consider himself as a separate being by the necessarily divisive character of thinking. It cannot be said what Brahman is, because the basic reality of the world does not belong in any class to which a word can be attached. Even though Brahman cannot be grasped in words and ideas, it can, however, be experienced, and the realization of this experience is the function of Yoga. This realization consists in the so-called unification of consciousness, that is, in the temporary renunciation of all divisive thinking and in the abandonment of all ideas and concepts about life. The world then may be experienced in its original, real, and inseparable state.

This type of experience is not, as might be supposed, sheer blank-mindedness, just as the concrete fact of nature is neither the collection of separate things that thought conceives nor mere empty space. If the student of comparative religions were to ask a Christian and a Vedantist for their ideas of what is ultimately real, the Vedantist would either be silent or say what is not, whereas the Christian would describe the positive attributes of God such as his love, wisdom, and intelligence. The student might therefore assume that the latter acknowledges a God who exists positively and the former a God who is almost nothing at all. He or she could conclude that Vedanta is a religion with an impoverished idea of God, failing to see that because it does not use the language of religion it cannot be a religion.

Two distinct ways of talking are used to characterize spiritual experiences. The religious way resembles trying to describe color to a blind person by saying what color may be compared to, for example, to variations of temperature. The way of liberation resembles trying to describe to the blind person what color is not. Both ways of speaking would be valid. A religion expresses the ultimate reality in particular terms such as those of human thought and imagination, and thus its view of God is determined and definite. A way of liberation sets thought aside in favor of direct experiencing and feeling, and thus its view is indeterminate and indefinite.

Buddhism.

Buddhism, the doctrine of Gautama Buddha, arose as a clarification and reform movement of Hinduism.

In many ways the objectives of Buddhism are the same as those of Vedanta and Yoga. Gautama Buddha avoided, however, giving even the barest name to that which is ultimately real, both in its universal aspect as Brahman and in its human aspect as the deepest self, or Atman. He felt that such terms were too easily turned into ideas and forms of thought that would detract from direct experience. His teaching was that people suffer because of *avidya*, or ignorance, of the total relativity of the world of things and events. Thought is *avidya* because it is a process of ignoring; that is, it cannot focus on any one aspect of experience without ignoring everything else. It is a way of looking at life bit by bit instead of totally and leads in turn to grasping (*trishna*, in Buddhism), or trying to wrest the desirable bits of experience away from the whole; however, because the good is always relative to the bad, this separation can never be accomplished. Similarly, one can never experience a solid without a surrounding space, space and solid being relative to each other. Giving up grasping leads to the Buddhist ideal of , which Gautama Buddha refused to define except in negative terms, as the Vedantist defines liberation.

47

Gautama Buddha's teaching led to a misunderstanding to which Vedanta is likewise prone, namely, that liberation may be sought as an escape from suffering, or as a permanent state of bliss. Later Buddhist leaders, especially those of the Mahayana school, corrected this misunderstanding by pointing out that seeking Nirvana as an escape was still grasping. Thus, their ideal of the wise individual went beyond the older Hindu view of leaving the world, that is, the social world, to prepare for death. It comprised returning into the full activity of society once liberated so that, free from fear, one could devote oneself to acts of compassion for those still in the bondage of *maya.* Buddhist teaching urges, however, morality and compassion not as a commandment but as voluntary action to which the free person commits himself or herself without hope of reward or fear of punishment. No thought is found in Buddhism of moral conduct as conformity to a divine pattern, for it considers moral standards like rules of grammar, that is, human conventions necessary for social existence but without any absolute authority.

Although Buddha gave no name to what he considered ultimate reality, later Buddhist teachers spoke of the true state of the world as *sunyata,* or "emptiness," meaning more exactly, "empty of any definable characteristic" or "unclassifiable." This philosophical attitude is in no sense equivalent to Western atheism or nihilism, for what is empty is not reality itself but every idea in which the human mind attempts to grasp it.

Expansion of Buddhism

Before its demise in India, Buddhism had already spread throughout Asia. This expansion started at least as early as the time of the emperor Asoka in the 3d century BC. According to tradition, this great monarch, who was himself a convert to Buddhism, actively supported the religion and sought to spread the dharma. He is said to have sent his own son, Mahinda, as a missionary to Sri Lanka (Ceylon). There Buddhism quickly took root and prospered, and the island was to become a stronghold of the Theravada sect. The Pali Canon was first written there in the 1st century BC; later the island was to be host to the great Theravadin systematizer and commentator Buddhaghosa (5th

48

century AD). Asoka is also said to have sent missionaries to the East to what is now Burma and Thailand. Whatever the truth of this claim, it is clear that by the first several centuries AD, Buddhism, accompanying the spread of Indian culture, had established itself in large areas of Southeast Asia, even as far as Indonesia.

Also, tradition has it that another son of Asoka established a Buddhist kingdom in central Asia. Whether or not this is true, it is clear that in subsequent centuries more missionaries (especially Mahayanists) followed the established trade routes west and north to this region, preaching the dharma as they went.

China

Central Asia was at that time a crossroads of creeds from all parts of Asia and the Near East, and by the 1st century AD Central Asian Buddhist monks were penetrating in turn into China. It is a matter of some debate what was transformed more in this process--China by Buddhism or Buddhism by China. On the one hand, at an early stage, Buddhists became very influential at the Chinese court, and soon their views penetrated the philosophical and literary circles of the gentry. On the other hand, early translators of Buddhist texts often adopted Taoist terminology in an attempt to make the Indian Buddhist concepts more understandable, and Buddhism adapted itself to Chinese world views, in particular to their stress on the importance of the family.

Buddhism in China also saw the rise of new sects, many of which were later transmitted to Japan. In the 6th century, the monk Chih-i consolidated the Tiantai school, which sought to order all Buddhist teachings into a set hierarchy culminating in the text known as the Lotus Sutra. During the Tang dynasty (618-907), the so-called golden age of Chinese Buddhism, the Huayan school (based on the teachings of the Avatamsaka sutra), the Faxiang school (which taught Vijnanavada doctrines and was promoted by the great pilgrim and scholar Xuanzang, and the Chan school (better known in Japan as Zen Buddhism) all prospered. At the same time, Pure Land Buddhism became increasingly popular.

By 845, however, the sangha had grown so large and rich that its tax-exempt status now made it a severe drain on the empire's economy. For this and other reasons it became the object of a brief but effective imperial persecution. Many temples were destroyed, thousands of monks and nuns were laicized, and the vast landholdings of monasteries were confiscated. Buddhism, especially the Chan school, did recover, but it never regained its former prestige in Chinese life.

Japan

Before 845, a number of Chinese schools had been transmitted to Japan. Buddhism was introduced to Japan from Korea about the 6th century and initially established itself as a superior means of magical power, especially for preserving and protecting the nation. Early in its history, it received the patronage of Prince Shotoku (7th century) and during the Nara period (710-84) became the state religion.

During the Heian period, in the early 9th century, two monks, Saicho and Kukai, traveled to China and on their return introduced to Japan the Tendai (or Chinese, Tiantai) sect and the Shingon sect, which was a form of Chinese Tantric Buddhism. Both of these esoteric sects were to take part in the mixing of Buddhism with various Japanese Shinto folk, ascetic, and magical practices. The Tendai sect, moreover, became a fountainhead of several later popular Japanese Buddhist movements. One of the Tendai's traits was the worship of the Buddha Amida and the belief in his Pure Land. With Honen (1133-1212) and Shinran (1173-1262), these Pure Land beliefs were systematized and made the exclusive focus of two new, popular sects, the Jodo and the Jodo Shin. Another Tendai trait was emphasis on the teachings of the Lotus Sutra. In the 13th century, the monk Nichiren founded a dynamic and nationalistic sect that made the Lotus its sole basis of worship. Finally, it was also in this same period that two schools of Zen Buddhism were introduced from China.

Under the feudal Tokugawa regime (1603-1867), all these sects became tools of the government; temples and priests were means of registering, educating, and controlling the populace. In the Meiji era (1868-1912), this Buddhist structure was disestablished in favor of Shinto. Finally, during the 20th century, new religious movements within Buddhism, such as the Soka-Gakkai and the Risshokosei-kai, have arisen in response to the problems of the modern age.

Taoism.

Attributed to the Chinese philosophers Lao-tzu and Chuang-tzu (fl. 4th cent. BC), Taoism is the specifically Chinese form of a way of liberation. In certain respects it resembles Buddhism, and Taoist terms were used liberally in translating Buddhist texts from Sanskrit into Chinese. Like Vedanta and Yoga, Taoism was adopted ordinarily by older men who had played their part in society according to the basic patterns of convention provided by Confucianism in China. In common with Mahayana Buddhism, Taoism allows for the return of the liberated sage into worldly affairs. Its principal text, the *Tao Tê Ching* (Teaching of Tao), attributed to Lao-tzu, was written as a manual of advice for rulers.

Taoism proper, as found in the teachings of Lao-tzu and Chuang-tzu, must be distinguished carefully from the so-called Taoist cult of divination, alchemy, and magic that is Taoist in nothing but name. Pure Taoism has never been organized and has remained the pursuit of independent scholars and philosophers both in China and Japan for more than 2000 years. It regards the natural universe as the operation of the Tao ("way"), which eludes all verbal and intellectual comprehension. Experience of the Tao is to be realized through *kuan* ("silent contemplation of nature") and *wu-wei* ("the absence of mental and physical strain"), which is equivalent to the Buddhist attitude of not grasping. Taoism emphasizes strongly the union of the individual and nature, suggesting that one controls the environment not by fighting it but by cooperating with it as a sailor uses the wind when tacking against it. Taoism is the philosophy underlying jujitsu, the so-called gentle way of defending oneself against an opponent by using the opponent's own strength to defeat him or her. Similarly, it teaches that one should control oneself by trusting rather than opposing one's natural feelings and instincts, by

51

channeling them in the directions in which one wants them to go rather than resisting them.

Confucianism

Confucianism, the philosophical system founded on the teaching of Confucius (551-479 BC), dominated Chinese sociopolitical life for most of Chinese history and largely influenced the cultures of Korea, Japan, and Indochina. The Confucian school functioned as a recruiting ground for government positions, which were filled by those scoring highest on examinations in the Confucian classics. It also blended with popular and imported religions and became the vehicle for articulating Chinese mores to the peasants. The school's doctrines supported political authority using the theory of the mandate of heaven. It sought to help the rulers maintain domestic order, preserve tradition, and maintain a constant standard of living for the taxpaying peasants. It trained its adherents in benevolence, traditional rituals, filial piety, loyalty, respect for superiors and for the aged, and principled flexibility in advising rulers.

Confucius

Westerners use Confucius as the spelling for K'ung Fu-tzu--Master K'ung-- China's first and most famous philosopher. Confucius had a traditional personal name (Ch'iu) and a formal name (Chung-ni). Confucius' father died shortly after Confucius' birth. His family fell into relative poverty, and Confucius joined a growing class of impoverished descendants of aristocrats who made their careers by acquiring knowledge of feudal ritual and taking positions of influence serving the rulers of the fragmented states of ancient China. Confucius devoted himself to learning. At age 30, however, when his short-lived official career floundered, he turned to teaching others. Confucius himself never wrote down his own philosophy, although tradition credits him with editing some of the historical classics that were used as texts in his school. He apparently made an enormous impact on the lives and attitudes of his disciples, however. The book known as the Analects, which records all that Confucius said was compiled by his students after his death. Because the Analects was not written as a systematic philosophy, it contains frequent contradictions and many of the philosophical doctrines are ambiguous. The Analects became the basis of the Chinese social lifestyle and the fundamental religious and philosophical point of view of most traditionalist Chinese intellectuals throughout history. The collection reveals Confucius as a person dedicated to the preservation of traditional ritual practices with an almost spiritual delight in performing ritual for its own sake.

Doctrine

Confucianism combines a political theory and a theory of human nature to yield a tao--a prescriptive doctrine or way. The political theory starts with a doctrine of political authority based on the mandate of heaven. The legitimate ruler derives authority from heaven's command. The ruler bears responsibility for the well-being of the people and therefore for peace and order in the empire.

Confucian philosophy presupposes a view of human nature in which humans are essentially social animals whose mode of social interaction is shaped by li (convention or ritual), which establishes value distinctions and prescribes activities in response to those distinctions. Education in li, or social rituals, is based on the natural behavioral propensity to imitate models. Sages, or superior people--those who have mastered the li--are the models of behavior from which the mass of people learn. Ideally, the ruler should himself be such a model and should appoint only those who are models of te (virtue) to positions of prominence. People are naturally inclined to emulate virtuous models; hence a hierarchy of merit results in widespread natural moral education.

Then, with practice, all people can in principle be like the sages, by acting in accordance with li without conscious effort. At that point they have acquired jen (humanity), the highest level of moral development; their natural inclinations are all in harmony with tao (way). The world is at peace, order abounds, and the harmony between the natural and the social sphere results in material well-being for everyone. This is Confucius' utopian vision, which he regards as modeled on the practice of the ancient sage kings.

Historical Development

Confucianism emerged as a more coherent philosophy when faced with intellectual competition from other schools that were growing in the fertile social upheavals of preimperial China (c.400-c.200 BC. Taoism, Mohism, and Legalism all attacked Confucianism. A common theme of these attacks was that Confucianism assumed that tradition or convention (li) was correct. Mencius (c.372-c.289 BC) developed a more idealistic version of Confucianism stressing jen as an innate inclination to good behavior that does not require education. Hsun Tzu (c.313-c.238 BC), on the contrary, argued that all inclinations are shaped by acquired language and other social forms.

Confucianism rose to the position of an official orthodoxy during the Han dynasty (206 BC-AD 220). It absorbed the metaphysical doctrines of Yin (the female principle) and Yang (the male principle) found in the I Ching (Book of Changes) and other speculative metaphysical notions. With the fall of the Han, the dynastic model, Confucianism fell into severe decline. Except for the residual effects of its official status, Confucianism lay philosophically dormant for about 600 years.

With the reestablishment of Chinese dynastic power in the T'ang dynasty (618-906) and the introduction of the Ch'an (Zen Buddhist) premise that "there is nothing much to Buddhist teaching," Confucianism began to revive. The Sung dynasty (960-1279) produced Neo-Confucianism--an interpretation of classical Confucian doctrine (principally that of Mencius) that addressed Buddhist and Taoist issues. The development of this philosophy was due mainly to Cheng-hao (1032-85) and Cheng-i (1033-1107), but for the orthodox statement of Neo-Confucianism, one turns to Chu Hsi (1130-1200). His commentaries on the four scriptures of Confucianism were required study for the imperial civil service examinations.

Neo-Confucianism focuses on the term li, which here means "lane" or "pattern." Correct behavior is held to follow a natural pattern (li) that is apprehended by hsin (heart-mind). Mencius' theory of the innate goodness of man is a theory of the innate ability of this heart-mind to apprehend li in situations and to follow it. To become a sage, one must study li and develop the ability to "see" it by a kind of intuition. Later, in the Ming dynasty (1368-1644), Wang Yang-Ming claimed that the heart projects li on things rather than just noticing external li. To become a sage, one cannot just study situations, one must act before li becomes manifest. Thus the heart-mind, which guides the action, is the source of li (moral patterns).

After the disastrous conflicts with Western military technology at the dawn of the 20th century, Chinese intellectuals blamed Confucianism for the scientific and political backwardness of China. Chinese Marxism, nonetheless, differs from Western Marxism in ways that reveal the persistence of Confucian attitudes toward politics, metaphysics, and theories of human psychology. Anti-Confucianism has been a theme in various political campaigns in modern China--most notably during and just after the Cultural Revolution. Increased toleration for all religions since Mao Tse-tung's death may lead to a moderate revival of Confucianism, although the interest seems to be mostly in historical issues.

In Taiwan, by contrast, Confucian orthodoxy has survived and serves to underpin an anti-Marxist, traditional authoritarianism. Serious, ongoing Confucian philosophy, however, is found mainly in Hong Kong and among Chinese scholars working in the West

China: History continued

China's northern border was long a zone of contact between the villagers to the south and the militaristic mounted nomads of the north. The Great Wall of China was begun during the Zhou dynasty(c.1027-256 B.C.) as a means of defense against the raiding nomads. During the Bronze Age, some aspects of Chinese civilization spread onto the Asian steppes from which these nomads came. Finely crafted bronze weapons and horse fittings have been found in great numbers in the Ordos (Mu Us) region of north central China. The earliest examples bear unmistakable resemblance to Shang bronzes. By the 1st century AD, the Ordos bronze style had acquired its own distinctive characteristics, including the vigorous portrayal of animals, often in combat. The nomads who produced these bronzes, although influenced by their neighbors to the south, must certainly have had their historical roots to the west, in the Central Asian steppes

The Iron Age appeared in China by about 600 BC, spreading widely during the course of the Warring States period (403-221 BC). This period also propelled new elements to positions of authority, as talent, not birth, increasingly became the criterion for employment. During this period of great upheaval, personal feudal relationships became outmoded, and a system of contractual relationships began to emerge. Bureaucrats, the forerunners of the Chinese scholar-official class, were given salaries, and peasants were expected to pay taxes to the government on their landholdings. The introduction of the ox-drawn, iron-tipped plow and the development of irrigation improved agricultural productivity and spurred population growth. A steady improvement in communications led to increased trade, and a money economy began to develop. The Chinese developed superior blast furnaces and technical apparatus with which to produce cast iron, techniques not employed in Europe until the Middle Ages. Early iron artifacts in China included swords and other weapons as well as implements of common use, such as axes, adzes, sickles, hoes, and other equipment that revolutionized Chinese agriculture. Following the Zhou dynasty, the warring states of China were unified into a single empire for the first time during the short-lived Qin (Ch'in) dynasty (221-206 BC).

The political unification of China during the latter half of the 3d century BC was accomplished by the western Wei He valley state of Qin (Ch'in). Having long been an effective opponent of the invaders from central Asia, the Qin armies adopted the nomad tactic of using mounted cavalry troops rather than the traditional Chinese chariots, a change that added greatly to their mobility. They captured the Zhou capital of Luoyang in 256 BC and reduced most of the central states to dependent status. From 230 to 221, under the able and unscrupulous Prince Zheng (Cheng), the Qin armies overcame all opposition; Zheng then assumed the imperial title of Shi Huangdi (Shih Huang-ti). His troops continued south as far as Guangdong (Kwangtung) and Guangxi (Kwangsi) and even into the Vietnamese border state of Tonkin. Shi Huangdi enlisted a vast Chinese labor force to complete the construction of the Great Wall of China along the

Mongolian border in the far north and also for the construction of extensive canal irrigation facilities in central China. The emperor tolerated no opposition, executing those who opposed his will and burning the books that scholars presumed to cite against him.

Shi Huangdi's premature death in 210 left control in the hands of a weak heir who was quite incapable of handling the problems he faced. Opposition factions, both feudal and scholarly, appeared in virtually every state and particularly in the Han region of the south. The Xiongnu (Hsiung-nu), Turkic bandits recently expelled from the north, returned to occupy the region from the Mongolian-Tibetan borders eastward to the Yellow Sea. The authority of Jin Shi's (Ch'in Shih's) successor collapsed in 206, and central power shifted to the Han dynasty.

Han dynasty (202 BC-AD 220) established a stable and highly centralized government on the Qin model, but it was somewhat more sensitive to the welfare of the peasantry, a perennial Confucian concern. The apogee of Han power was reached under Han Wudi, the "Martial Emperor" (r. 140-87 BC), who waged war against the nomadic tribes to the north, moved westward to Central Asia to gain control of the Silk Road upon which goods passed between China and the Roman world, and established a Chinese colony in northern Korea.

Han dealings with barbarian neighbors, as well as subsequent Chinese relations with these peoples, were conducted within the tribute system. Under this system China granted diplomatic recognition and trading privileges only to those states and peoples acknowledging its superiority, symbolized by a payment of tribute. If Qin saw the triumph of Legalism, Han saw the advancement of Confucian doctrine to preeminence in the state. Bureaucratic candidates were examined in Confucian wisdom, fulfilling the Confucian dictum that only morally superior men were fit for office. Under the Han, China began to outstrip other world civilizations in technology, developing the first true paper, protoporcelain, and a primitive seismograph.

The end of the Han came largely as the result of economic woes--powerful landlords had shifted too much land from the tax rolls, thereby making unbearable the increased burden on the poorer farmers--and intense political factionalism at the imperial court. The resulting economic hardships and governmental disintegration led to massive peasant rebellion and the dissolution of the empire. Then commenced 300 years of political fragmentation known as the Period of Disunion (220-589), during which North China was ruled by a series of semi-Sinicized barbarian peoples and the South was settled by Chinese colonial regimes. With the breakdown of the Han order came a disillusionment with Confucian emphasis on the selection of morally upright men for office and a return to aristocratic domination of government. Although the period was one of deteriorating administrative quality, fierce racial tensions, and considerable physical destruction, it was also notable for institutional and cultural developments, especially the transformation of Indian Buddhism into a Chinese religion. Technological innovations included the invention of the wheelbarrow and gunpowder.

AFRICAN HISTORY
PRIMARY SOURCES
TO 1500 A.D.

Herodotus: *The Histories*, c. 430 BCE, Book III.

I went as far as Elephantine [Aswan] to see what I could with my own eyes, but for the country still further south I had to be content with what I was told in answer to my questions. South of Elephantine the country is inhabited by Ethiopians...Beyond the island is a great lake, and round its shores live nomadic tribes of Ethiopians. After crossing the lake one comes again to the stream of the Nile, which flows into it. ...After forty days journey on land along the river, one takes another boat and in twelve days reaches a big city named Meroë, said to be the capital city of the Ethiopians. The inhabitants worship Zeus and Dionysus alone of the Gods, holding them in great honor. There is an oracle of Zeus there, and they make war according to its pronouncements, taking it from both the occasion and the object of their various expeditions. . . .After this Cambyses [King of Persia] took counsel with himself, and planned three expeditions. One was against the Carthaginians, another against the Ammonians, and a third against the long-lived Ethiopians, who dwelt in that part of Libya which borders upon the southern sea. . . while his spies went into Ethiopia, under the pretense of carrying presents to the king, but in reality to take note of all they saw, and especially to observe whether there was really what is called "the table of the Sun" in Ethiopia. Now the table of the Sun according to the accounts given of it may be thus described: It is a meadow in the skirts of their city full of the boiled flesh of all manner of beasts, which the magistrates are careful to store with meat every night, and where whoever likes may come and eat during the day. The people of the land say that the earth itself brings forth the food. Such is the description which is given of this table.

The Ethiopians to whom this embassy was sent are said to be the tallest and handsomest men in the whole world. In their customs they differ greatly from the rest of mankind, and particularly in the way they choose their kings; for they find out the man who is the tallest of all the citizens, and of strength equal to his height, and appoint him to rule over them....The spies were told that most of them lived to be a hundred and twenty years old, while some even went beyond that age---they ate boiled flesh, and had for their drink nothing but milk. Among these Ethiopians copper is of all metals the most scarce and valuable. Also, last of all, they were allowed to behold the coffins of the Ethiopians, which are made (according to report) of crystal, after the following fashion: When the dead body has been dried, either in the Egyptian, or in some other manner, they cover the whole with gypsum, and adorn it with painting until it is as like the living man as possible. Then they place the body in a crystal pillar which has been hollowed out to receive it, crystal being dug up in great abundance in their country, and of a kind very easy to work. You may see the corpse through the pillar within which it lies; and it neither gives out any unpleasant odor, nor is it in any respect unseemly; yet there is no part that is not as plainly visible as if the body were bare. The next of kin keep the crystal pillar in their houses for a full year from the time of the death, and give it the first fruits continually, and honor it with sacrifice. After the year is out they bear the pillar forth, and set it up near the town. . . .

Where the south declines towards the setting sun lies the country called Ethiopia, the last inhabited land in that direction. There gold is obtained in great plenty, huge elephants abound, with wild trees of all sorts, and ebony; and the men are taller, handsomer, and longer lived than anywhere else. The Ethiopians were clothed in the skins of leopards and lions, and had long bows made of the stem of the palm-leaf, not less than four cubits in length. On these they laid short arrows made of reed, and armed at the tip, not with iron, but with a piece of stone, sharpened to a point, of the kind used in engraving seals. They carried likewise spears, the head of which was the sharpened horn of an antelope; and in addition they had knotted clubs. When they went into battle they painted their bodies, half with chalk, and half with vermilion. . . .

Acts of the Apostles 8:26-39, *The Bible*, c. 90 A.D.

Then the angel of the Lord spoke to Philip, "Get up and head south on the road that goes down from Jerusalem to Gaza, the desert route." So he got up and set out. Now there was an Ethiopian eunuch, a court official of the Candace, that is, the queen of the Ethiopians, in charge of here entire treasury, who had come to Jerusalem to worship, and was returning home. Seated in his chariot, he was reading the prophet Isaiah. The Spirit said to Philip, "Go and join up with that chariot." Philip ran up and heard him reading Isaiah the prophet and said, "Do you understand what you are reading?" He replied, "How can I, unless someone instructs me?" So he invited Philip to get in and sit with him. This was the scripture passage he was reading: Like a sheep he was led to the slaughter, and as a lamb before its shearer is silent, so he opened not his mouth. In his humiliation justice was denied him. Who will tell of his posterity? For his life is taken from the earth. Then the eunuch said to Philip in reply, "I beg you, about whom is the prophet saying this? About himself, or about someone else?" Then Philip opened his mouth and, beginning with this scripture passage, he proclaimed Jesus to him. As they traveled along the road they came to some water, and the eunuch said, "Look, there is water. What is to prevent my being baptized?" Then he ordered the chariot to stop, and Philip and the eunuch both went down into the water, and he baptized him. When they came out of the water, the Spirit of the Lord snatched Philip away, and the eunuch saw him no more, but continued on his way rejoicing.

Dio Cassius: *History of Rome*, c. 220 CE
Book LIV.v.4-6.

About this same time [23 B.C.] the Ethiopians, who dwell beyond Egypt, advanced as far as the city called Elephantine, with the Candace as their leader, ravaging everything they encountered. At Elephantine, however, learning that Gaius Petronius, the governor of Egypt, was already moving, they hastily retreated before he arrived, hoping to make good their escape. But being overtaken on the road, they were defeated and thus drew him after them into their own country. There, too, he fought successfully with them, and took Napata, their capital, among other cities. This place was razed to the ground, and a garrison left at another point; for Petronius, finding himself unable either to advance farther, on account of the sand and the heat, or advantageously to remain where he was with his entire army, withdrew, taking the greater part of it with him. Thereupon the Ethiopians attacked the garrisons, but he again proceeded against them, rescued his own men, and compelled the Candace to make terms with him.

Inscription of Ezana, King of Axum, c. 325 CE

Through the might of the Lord of All I took the field against the Noba [Nubians] when the people of Noba revolted, when they boasted and "He will not cross over the Takkaze," said the Noba, when they did violence to the peoples Mangurto and Hasa and Barya, and the Black Noba waged war on the Red Noba and a second and a third time broke their oath and without consideration slew their neighbors and plundered our envoys and messengers whom I had sent to interrogate them, robbing them of their possessions and seizing their lances. When I sent again and they did not hear me, and reviled me, and made off, I took the field against them. And I armed myself with the power of the Lord of the Land and fought on the Takkaze at the ford of Kemalke. And thereupon they fled and stood not still, and I pursued the fugitives twenty-three days slaying them and capturing others and taking plunder from them, where I came; while prisoners and plunder were brought back by my own people who marched out; while I burnt their towns, those of masonry and those of straw, and seized their corn and their bronze and the dried meat and the images in their temples and destroyed the stocks of corn and cotton; and the enemy plunged into the river Seda, and many perished in the water, the number I know not, and as their vessels foundered a multitude of people, men and women were drowned. . .

And I arrived at the Kasu [Kush], slaying them and taking others prisoner at the junction of the rivers Seda and Takkaze. And on the day after my arrival I dispatched into the field the troop of Mahaza and the Damawa and Falha and Sera up the Seda against the towns of masonry and of straw; their towns of masonry are called Alwa, Daro. And they slew and took prisoners and threw them into the water and they returned safe and sound, after they had terrified their enemies and had conquered through the power of the Lord of the Land. And I sent the troop Halen and the troop Laken and the troop Sabarat and Falha and Sera down the Seda against the towns of straw of the Noba and Negues; the towns of masonry of the Kasu which the Noba had taken were Tabito, Fertoti; and they arrived at the territory of the Red Noba, and my people returned safe and sound after they had taken prisoners and slain others and had seized their plunder through the power of the Lord of Heaven. And I erected a throne at the junction of the rivers Seda and Takkaze, opposite the town of masonry which is on this peninsula.

Procopius of Caesarea: *History of the Wars*, **c. 550 CE**

Book I.xix.1, 17-22, 27-37, xx.1-13

At that time the idea occurred to the Emperor Justinian to ally himself with the Ethiopians and the Omeritae, in order to injure the Persians. . . .About opposite the Omeritae on the opposite mainland dwell the Ethiopians who are called Auxumitae, because their king resides in the city of Auxomis [Axum]. And the expanse of sea which lies between is crossed in a voyage of five days and nights, when a moderately favoring wind blows. . . .

From the city of Auxumis to the Egyptian boundaries of the Roman domain, where the city called Elephantine is situated, is a journey of thirty days for an unencumbered traveler. Within that space many nations are settled, and among them the Blemmyae and the Nobatae [Nubians], who are very large nations. But the Blemmyae dwell in the central portion of the country, while the Nobatae possess the territory about the River Nile. Formerly this was not the limit of the Roman Empire, but it lay beyond there as far as one would advance in a seven days' journey; but the Roman Emperor Diocletian came there, and observed that the tribute from these places was of the smallest possible account, since the land is at that point extremely narrow (for rocks rise to an exceedingly great height at no great distance from the Nile and spread over the rest of the country), while a very large body of soldiers had been stationed there from of old, the maintenance of which was an excessive burden upon the public; and at the same time the Nobatae who formerly dwelt about the city of Premnis [modern Karanog--now submerged beneath Lake Nasser] used to plunder the whole region; so he persuaded these barbarians to move from their own habitations, and to settle along the River Nile, promising to bestow upon them great cities and land both extensive and incomparably better than that which they had previously occupied. For in this way he thought that they would no longer harass the country about Pselchis [modern Maharraqa--now submerged beneath Lake Nasser] at least, and that they would possess themselves of the land given them, as being their own, and would probably beat off the Blemmyae and the other barbarians.

And since this pleased the Nobatae, they made the migration immediately, just as Diocletian directed them, and took possession of all the Roman cities and the land on both sides of the River beyond the city of Elephantine. Then it was that this emperor decreed that to them and to the Blemmyae a fixed sum of gold should be given every year with the stipulation that they should no longer plunder the land of the Romans. And they receive this gold even up to my time, but none the less they overrun the country there. Thus, it seems that with all barbarians there is no means of compelling them to keep faith with the Romans except through the fear of soldiers to hold them in check. And yet this emperor went so far as to select a certain island in the River Nile close to the city of Elephantine and there construct a very strong fortress in which he established certain temples and altars for the Romans and these barbarians in common, and he settled priests of both nations in this fortress, thinking that the friendship between them would be secure by reason of their sharing the things sacred to them. And for this reason he named the place Philae. Now, both these nations, the Blemmyae and the Nobatae, believe in all the gods in which the Greeks believe, and they also reverence Isis and Osiris, and not least of all Priapus. But the Blemmyae are accustomed also to sacrifice human beings to the Sun. These sanctuaries in Philae were kept by these barbarians even up to my time, but the Emperor Justinian decided to tear them down. . . .

At about the time of this war Ellestheaeus, the king of the Ethiopians, who was a Christian and a most devoted adherent of this faith, discovered that a number of the >Omeritae on the opposite mainland [modern Yemen] were oppressing the Christians there outrageously; many of these rascals were Jews, and many of them held in reverence the old faith which men of the present day call Hellenic [i.e., pagan]. He therefore collected a fleet of ships and an army and came against them, and he conquered them in battle and slew both the king and many of the Omeritae. He then set up in his stead a Christian king, an Omeritae by birth, by name Esimiphaeus, and, after ordaining that he should pay a tribute to the Ethiopians every year, he returned to his home. In this

Ethiopian army many slaves and all who were readily disposed to crime were quite unwilling to follow the king back, but were left behind and remained there because of their desire for the land of the Omeritae; for it is an extremely goodly land.

These fellows at a time not long after this, in company with certain others, rose against the king Esimiphaeus and put him in confinement in one of the fortresses there, and established another king over the Omeritae, Abramus by name. Now this Abramus was a Christian, but a slave of a Roman citizen who was engaged in the business of shipping in the city of Adulis in Ethiopia. When Ellestheaeus learned this, he was eager to punish Abramus together with those who had revolted with him for their injustice to Esimiphaeus, and he sent against them an army of three thousand men with one of his relatives as commander. This army, once there, was no longer willing to return home, but they wished to remain where they were in a goodly land, and so without the knowledge of their commander they opened negotiations with Abramus; then when they came to an engagement with their opponents, just as the fighting began, they killed their commander and joined the ranks of the enemy, and so remained there. But Ellestheaeus was greatly moved with anger and sent still another army against them; this force engaged with Abramus and his men, and, after suffering a severe defeat in the battle, straightway returned home. Thereafter the king of the Ethiopians became afraid, and sent no further expeditions against Abramus. After the death of Ellestheaeus, Abramus agreed to pay tribute to the king of the Ethiopians who succeeded him, and in this way he strengthened his rule. But this happened at a later time.

At that time, when Ellestheaeus was reigning over the Ethiopians, and Esimiphaeus over the Omeritae, the Emperor Justinian sent an ambassador, Julianus, demanding that both nations on account of their community of religion should make common cause with the Romans in the war against the Persians; for he purposed that the Ethiopians, by purchasing silk from India and selling it among the Romans, might themselves gain much money, while cause the Romans to profit in only one way, namely, that they be no longer compelled to pay over their money to their enemy (this is the silk of which they are accustomed to make the garments which of old the Greeks called

"Medic," but which at the present time they name "Seric" [from Lat. serica, as coming from the Chinese (Seres)]. As for the Omeritae, it was desired that they should establish Caïsus, the fugitive, as captain over the Maddeni, and with a great army of their own people and of the Maddene Saracens make an invasion into the land of the Persians. This Caïsus was by birth of the captain's rank and an exceptionally able warrior, but he had killed one of the relativesof Esimiphaeus and was a fugitive in a land which is utterly destitute of human habitation.

So each king, promising to put this demand into effect, dismissed the ambassador, but neither one of them did the things agreed upon by them. For it was impossible for the Ethiopians to buy silk from the Indians, for the Persian merchants always locate themselves at the very harbors where the Indian ships first put in (since they inhabit the adjoining country), and are accustomed to buy the whole cargoes; and it seemed to the Omeritae a difficult thing to cross a country which was a desert and which extended so far that a long time was required for the journey across it, and then to go against such a people much more warlike than themselves. Later on Abramus too, when at length he had established his power most securely, promised the Emperor Justinian many times to invade the land of Persia, but only once began the journey and then straightway turned back. Such then were the relations which the Romans had with the Ethiopians and the Omeritae.

Herodotus: *The Histories*, c. 430 B.C., Book IV.42-43:

For my part I am astonished that men should ever have divided Libya, Asia, and Europe as they have, for they are exceedingly unequal. Europe extends the entire length of the other two, and for breadth will not even (as I think) bear to be compared to them. As for Libya, we know it to be washed on all sides by the sea, except where it is attached to Asia. This discovery was first made by Necos, the Egyptian king, who on desisting from the canal which he had begun between the Nile and the Arabian gulf [i.e., the Red Sea], sent to sea a number of ships manned by Phoenicians, with orders to make for the Pillars of Hercules, and return to Egypt through them, and by the Mediterranean. The Phoenicians took their departure from Egypt by way of the Erythraean sea, and so sailed into the southern ocean. When autumn came, they went ashore, wherever they might happen to be, and having sown a tract of land with corn, waited until the grain was fit to cut. Having reaped it, they again set sail; and thus it came to pass that two whole years went by, and it was not till the third year that they doubled the Pillars of Hercules, and made good their voyage home. On their return, they declared - I for my part do not believe them, but perhaps others may - that in sailing round Libya they had the sun upon their right hand. In this way was the extent of Libya first discovered.

Next to these Phoenicians the Carthaginians, according to their own accounts, made the voyage. For Sataspes, son of Teaspes the Achaemenian, did not circumnavigate Libya, though he was sent to do so; but, fearing the length and desolateness of the journey, he turned back and left unaccomplished the task which had been set him by his mother. This man had used violence towards a maiden, the daughter of Zopyrus, son of Megabyzus, and King Xerxes was about to impale him for the offence, when his mother, who was a sister of Darius, begged him off, undertaking to punish his crime more heavily than the king himself had designed. She would force him, she said, to sail round Libya and return to Egypt by the Arabian gulf. Xerxes gave his consent; and Sataspes went down to Egypt, and there got a ship and crew, with which he set sail for the Pillars of Hercules. Having passed the Straits, he doubled the Libyan headland, known as Cape Soloeis, and proceeded southward.

Following this course for many months over a vast stretch of sea, and finding that more water than he had crossed still lay ever before him, he put about, and came back to Egypt. Thence proceeding to the court, he made report to Xerxes, that at the farthest point to which he had reached, the coast was occupied by a dwarfish race, who wore a dress made from the palm tree. These people, whenever he landed, left their towns and fled away to the mountains; his men, however, did them no wrong, only entering into their cities and taking some of their cattle. The reason why he had not sailed quite round Libya was, he said, because the ship stopped, and would no go any further. Xerxes, however, did not accept this account for true; and so Sataspes, as he had failed to accomplish the task set him, was impaled by the king's orders in accordance with the former sentence.

Book IV.168-198:

The Libyans dwell in the order which I will now describe. Beginning on the side of Egypt, the first Libyans are the Adyrmachidae. These people have, in most points, the same customs as the Egyptians, but use the costume of the Libyans. Their women wear on each leg a ring made of bronze; they let their hair grow long, and when they catch any vermin on their persons, bite it and throw it away. In this they differ from all the other Libyans. They are also the only tribe with whom the custom obtains of bringing all women about to become brides before the king, that he may choose such as are agreeable to him. The Adyrmachidae extend from the borders of Egypt to the harbor called Port Plynus. Next to the Adyrmachidae are the Gilligammae, who inhabit the country westward as far as the island of Aphrodisias. Off this tract is the island of Platea, which the Cyrenaeans colonized. Here too, upon the mainland, are Port Menelaus, and Aziris, where the Cyrenaeans once lived. The Silphium begins to grow in this region, extending from the island of Platea on the one side to the mouth of the Syrtis on the other. The customs of the Gilligammae are like those of the rest of their countrymen.

The Asbystae adjoin the Gilligammae upon the west. They inhabit the regions above Cyrene, but do not reach to the coast, which belongs to the Cyrenaeans. Four-horse chariots are in more common use among them than among any other Libyans. In most of their customs they ape the manners of the Cyrenaeans. Westward of the Asbystae dwell the Auschisae, who possess the country above Barca, reaching, however, to the sea at the place called Euesperides. In the middle of their territory is the little tribe of the Cabalians, which touches the coast near Tauchira, a city of the Barcaeans. Their customs are like those of the Libyans above Cyrene.

The Nasamonians, a numerous people, are the western neighbors of the Auschisae. In summer they leave their flocks and herds upon the sea-shore, and go up the country to a place called Augila, where they gather the dates from the palms, which in those parts grow thickly, and are of great size, all of them being of the fruit-bearing kind. They also chase the locusts, and, when caught, dry them in the sun, after which they grind them to powder, and, sprinkling this upon their milk, so drink it. Each man among them has several wives, in their intercourse with whom they resemble the Massagetae. The following are their customs in the swearing of oaths and the practice of augury. The man, as he swears, lays his hand upon the tomb of some one considered to have been pre-eminently just and good, and so doing swears by his name. For divination they betake themselves to the sepulchers of their own ancestors, and, after praying, lie down to sleep upon their graves; by the dreams which then come to them they guide their conduct. When they pledge their faith to one another, each gives the other to drink out of his hand; if there be no liquid to be had, they take up dust from the ground, and put their tongues to it.

On the country of the Nasamonians borders that of the Psylli, who were swept away under the following circumstances. The south-wind had blown for a long time and dried up all the tanks in which their water was stored. Now the whole region within the Syrtis is utterly devoid of springs. Accordingly the Psylli took counsel among themselves, and by common consent made war upon the southwind---so at least the Libyans say, I do but repeat their words---they went forth and reached the desert; but there the south-wind rose and buried them under heaps of sand: whereupon, the Psylli being destroyed, their lands passed to the Nasamonians.

Above the Nasamonians, towards the south, in the district where the wild beasts abound, dwell the Garamantians, who avoid all society or intercourse with their fellow-men, have no weapon of war, and do not know how to defend themselves. These border the Nasamonians on the south: westward along the sea-shore their neighbors are the

Macea, who, by letting the locks about the crown of their head grow long, while they clip them close everywhere else, make their hair resemble a crest. In war these people use the skins of ostriches for shields. The river Cinyps rises among them from the height called "the Hill of the Graces," and runs from thence through their country to the sea. The Hill of the Graces is thickly covered with wood, and is thus very unlike the rest of Libya, which is bare. It is distant two hundred furlongs from the sea. Adjoining the Macae are the Gindanes, whose women wear on their legs anklets of leather. Each lover that a woman has gives her one; and she who can show the most is the best esteemed, as she appears to have been loved by the greatest number of men.

A promontory jutting out into the sea from the country of the Gindanes is inhabited by the Lotophagi, who live entirely on the fruit of the lotus-tree. The lotus fruit is about the size of the lentisk berry, and in sweetness resembles the date. The Lotophagi even succeed in obtaining from it a sort of wine. The sea-coast beyond the Lotophagi is occupied by the Machlyans, who use the lotus to some extent, though not so much as the people of whom we last spoke. The Machlyans reach as far as the great river called the Triton, which empties itself into the great lake Tritonis. Here, in this lake, is an island called Phla, which it is said the Lacedaemonians were to have colonized, according to an oracle.

The following is the story as it is commonly told. When Jason had finished building the Argo at the foot of Mount Pelion, he took on board the usual hecatomb, and moreover a brazen tripod. Thus equipped, he set sail, intending to coast round the Peloponnese, and so to reach Delphi. The voyage was prosperous as far as Malea; but at that point a gale of wind from the north came on suddenly, and carried him out of his course to the coast of Libya; where, before he discovered the land, he got among the shallows of Lake Tritonis. As he was turning it in his mind how he should find his way out, Triton (they say) appeared to him, and offered to show him the channel, and secure him a safe retreat, if he would give him the tripod. Jason complying, was shown by Triton the passage through the shallows; after which the god took the tripod, and, carrying it to his own temple, seated himself upon it, and, filled with prophetic fury, delivered to Jason and his companions a long prediction. "When a descendant," he said, "of one of the Argo's crew should seize and carry off the brazen tripod, then by inevitable fate would a hundred Grecian cities be built around Lake Tritonis." The Libyans of that region, when they heard the words of this prophecy, took away the tripod and hid it.

The next tribe beyond the Machlyans is the tribe of the Auseans. Both these nations inhabit the borders of Lake Tritonis, being separated from one another by the river Triton. Both also wear their hair long, but the Machlyans let it grow at the back of the head, while the Auseans have it long in front. The Ausean maidens keep year by year a feast in honor of Minerva, whereat their custom is to draw up in two bodies, and fight with stones and clubs. They say that these are rites which have come down to them from their fathers, and that they honor with them their native goddess, who is the same as the Minerva (Athena) of the Grecians. If any of the maidens die of the wounds they receive, the Auseans declare that such are false maidens. Before the fight is suffered to begin, they have another ceremony. One of the virgins, the loveliest of the number, is selected from the rest; a Corinthian helmet and a complete suit of Greek armor are publicly put upon her; and, thus adorned, she is made to mount into a chariot, and led around the whole lake in a procession. What arms they used for the adornment of their damsels before the Greeks came to live in their country, I cannot say. I imagine they dressed them in Egyptian armor, for I maintain that both the shield and the helmet came into Greece from Egypt. The Auseans declare that Minerva is the daughter of Neptune and the Lake Tritonis---they say she quarreled with her father, and applied to Jupiter, who consented to let her be his child; and so she became his adopted daughter. These people do not marry or live in families, but dwell together like the gregarious beasts. When their children are full-grown, they are brought before the assembly of the men, which is held every third month, and assigned to those whom they most resemble.

Such are the tribes of wandering Libyans dwelling upon the sea-coast. Above them inland is the wild-beast tract: and beyond that, a ridge of sand, reaching from Egyptian Thebes to the Pillars of Hercules. Throughout this ridge, at the distance of about ten days' journey from one another, heaps of salt in large lumps lie upon hills. At the top of every hill there gushes forth from the middle of the salt a stream of water, which is both cold and sweet. Around dwell men who are the last inhabitants of Libya on the side of the desert, living, as they do, more inland than the wild-beast district. Of these nations the first is that of the Ammonians, who dwell at a distance of ten days' from Thebes [Waset], and have a temple derived from that of the Theban Jupiter. For at Thebes likewise, as I mentioned above, the image of Jupiter has a face like that of a ram. The Ammonians have another spring besides that which rises from the salt. The water of this stream is lukewarm at early dawn; at the time when the market fills it is much cooler; by noon it has grown quite cold; at this time, therefore, they water their gardens. As the afternoon advances the coldness goes off, till, about sunset, the water is once more lukewarm; still the heat increases, and at midnight it boils furiously. After this time it again begins to cool, and grows less and less hot till morning comes. This spring is called "the Fountain of the Sun." Next to the Ammonians, at the distance of ten days' journey along the ridge of sand, there is a second salt-hill like the Ammonian, and a second spring. The country round is inhabited, and the place bears the name of Augila. Hither it is that the Nasamonians come to gather in the dates.

Ten days' journey from Augila there is again a salt-hill and a spring; palms of the fruitful kind grow here abundantly, as they do also at the other salt-hills. This region is inhabited by a nation called the Garamantians, a very powerful people, who cover the salt with mold, and then sow their crops. From thence is the shortest road to the Lutophagi, a journey of thirty days. In the Garamantian country are found the oxen which, as they graze, walk backwards. This they do because their horns curve outwards in front of their heads, so that it is not possible for them when grazing to move forwards, since in that case their horns would become fixed in the ground. Only herein do they differ from other oxen, and further in the thickness and hardness of their hides. The Garamantians have four-horse chariots, in which they chase the Troglodyte Ethiopians, who of all the nations whereof any account has reached our ears are by far the swiftest of foot. The Troglodytes feed on serpents, lizards, and other similar reptiles. Their language is unlike that of any other people; it sounds like the screeching of bats.

At the distance of ten days' journey from the Garamantians there is again another salt-hill and spring of water; around which dwell a people, called the Atarantians, who alone of all known nations are destitute of names. The title of Atarantians is borne by the whole race in common; but the men have no particular names of their own. The Atarantians, when the sun rises high in the heaven, curse him, and load him with reproaches, because (they say) he burns and wastes both their country and themselves. Once more at the distance of ten days' there is a salt-hill, a spring, and an inhabited tract. Near the salt is a mountain called Atlas, very taper and round; so lofty, moreover, that the top (it is said) cannot be seen, the clouds never quitting it either summer or winter. The natives call this mountain "the Pillar of Heaven"; and they themselves take their name from it, being called Atlantes. They are reported not to eat any living thing, and never to have any dreams.

As far as the Atlantes the names of the nations inhabiting the sandy ridge are known to me; but beyond them my knowledge fails. The ridge itself extends as far as the Pillars of Hercules, and even further than these; and throughout the whole distance, at the end of every ten days' there is a salt-mine, with people dwelling round it who all of them build their houses with blocks of the salt. No rain falls in these parts of Libya; if it were otherwise, the walls of these houses could not stand. The salt quarried is of two colors, white and purple. Beyond the ridge, southwards, in the direction of the interior, the country is a desert, with no springs, no beasts, no rain, no wood, and altogether destitute of moisture.

Thus from Egypt as far as Lake Tritonis Libya is inhabited by wandering tribes, whose drink is milk and their food the flesh of animals. Cow's flesh, however, none of these tribes ever taste, but abstain from it for the same reason as the Egyptians, neither do they any of them breed swine. Even at Cyrene, the women think it wrong to eat the flesh of the cow, honoring in this Isis, the Egyptian goddess, whom they worship both with fasts and festivals. The Barcaean women abstain, not from cow's flesh only, but also from the flesh of swine. West of Lake Tritonis the Libyans are no longer wanderers, nor do they practice the same customs as the wandering people, or treat their children in the same way. For the wandering Libyans, many of them at any rate, if not all---concerning which I cannot speak with certainty---when their children come to the age of four years, burn the veins at the top of their heads with a flock from the fleece of a sheep: others burn the veins about the temples. This they do to prevent them from being plagued in their after lives by a flow of rheum from the head; and such they declare is the reason why they are so much more healthy than other men. Certainly the Libyans are the healthiest men that I know; but whether this is what makes them so, or not, I cannot positively say---the healthiest certainly they are. If when the children are being burnt convulsions come on, there is a remedy of which they have made discovery. It is to sprinkle goat's water upon the child, who thus treated, is sure to recover. In all this I only repeat what is said by the Libyans.

The rites which the wandering Libyans use in sacrificing are the following. They begin with the ear of the victim, which they cut off and throw over their house: this done, they kill the animal by twisting the neck. They sacrifice to the Sun and Moon, but not to any other god. This worship is common to all the Libyans. The inhabitants of the parts about Lake Tritonis worship in addition Triton, Neptune, and Minerva, the last especially. The dress wherewith Minerva's statues are adorned, and her Aegis, were derived by the Greeks from the women of Libya. For, except that the garments of the Libyan women are of leather, and their fringes made of leathern thongs instead of serpents, in all else the dress of both is exactly alike. The name too itself shows that the mode of dressing the Pallas-statues came from Libya. For the Libyan women wear over their dress stripped of the hair, fringed at their edges, and colored with vermilion; and from these goat-skins the Greeks get their word Aegis (goat-harness). I think for my part that the loud cries uttered in our sacred rites came also from thence; for the Libyan women are greatly given to such cries and utter them very sweetly. Likewise the Greeks learnt from the Libyans to yoke four horses to a chariot.

All the wandering tribes bury their dead according to the fashion of the Greeks, except the Nasamonians. They bury them sitting, and are right careful when the sick man is at the point of giving up the ghost, to make him sit and not let him die lying down. The dwellings of these people are made of the stems of the asphodel, and of rushes wattled together. They can be carried from place to place. Such are the customs of the afore-mentioned tribes.

Westward of the river Triton and adjoining upon the Auseans, are other Libyans who till the ground, and live in houses: these people are named the Maxyans. They let the hair grow long on the right side of their heads, and shave it close on the left; they besmear their bodies with red paint; and they say that they are descended from the men of Troy. Their country and the remainder of Libya towards the west is far fuller of wild beasts and of wood than the country of the wandering people. For the eastern side of Libya, where the wanderers dwell, is low and sandy, as far as the river Triton; but westward of that the land of the husbandmen is very hilly, and abounds with forests and wild beasts. For this is the tract in which the huge serpents are found, and the lions, the elephants, the bears, the aspics, and the horned asses. Here too are the dog-faced creatures, and the creatures without heads, whom the Libyans declare to have their eyes in their breasts; and also the wild men, and wild women, and many other far less fabulous beasts.

Among the wanderers are none of these, but quite other animals; as antelopes, gazelles, buffaloes, and asses, not of the horned sort, but of a kind which does not need to drink; also oryxes, whose horns are used for the curved sides of citherns, and whose size is about that of the ox; foxes, hyaenas porcupines, wild rams, dictyes, jackals, panthers, boryes, land-crocodiles about three cubits in length, very like lizards, ostriches, and little snakes, each with a single horn. All these animals are found here, and likewise those belonging to other countries, except the stag and the wild boar; but neither stag nor wild-boar are found in any part of Libya. There are, however, three sorts of mice in these parts; the first are called two-footed; the next, zegeries, which is a Libyan word meaning "hills"; and the third, urchins. Weasels also are found in the Silphium region, much like the Tartessian. So many, therefore, are the animals belonging to the land of the wandering Libyans, in so far at least as my researches have been able to reach.

Next to the Maxyan Libyans are the Zavecians, whose wives drive their chariots to battle. On them border the Gyzantians; in whose country a vast deal of honey is made by bees; very much more, however, by the skill of men. The people all paint themselves red, and eat monkeys, whereof there is inexhaustible store in the hills. Off their coast, as the Carthaginians report, lies an island, by name Cyraunis, the length of which is two hundred furlongs, its breadth not great, and which is soon reached from the mainland. Vines and olive trees cover the whole of it, and there is in the island a lake, from which the young maidens of the country draw up gold-dust, by dipping into the mud birds' feathers smeared with pitch. If this be true, I know not; I but write what is said. It may be even so, however; since I myself have seen pitch drawn up out of the water from a lake in Zacynthus. At the place I speak of there are a number of lakes; but one is larger than the rest, being seventy feet every way, and two fathoms in depth. Here they let down a pole into the water, with a bunch of myrtle tied to one end, and when they raise it again, there is pitch sticking to the myrtle, which in smell is like to bitumen, but in all else is better than the pitch of Pieria. This they pour into a trench dug by the lake's side; and when a good deal has thus been got together, they draw it off and put it up in jars. Whatever falls into the lake passes underground, and comes up in the sea, which is no less than four furlongs distant. So then what is said of the island off the Libyan coast is not without likelihood.

The Carthaginians also relate the following: There is a country in Libya, and a nation, beyond the Pillars of Hercules, which they are wont to visit, where they no sooner arrive but forthwith they unlade their wares, and, having disposed them after an orderly fashion along the beach, leave them, and, returning aboard their ships, raise a great smoke. The natives, when they see the smoke, come down to the shore, and, laying out to view so much gold as they think the worth of the wares, withdraw to a distance. The Carthaginians upon this come ashore and look. If they think the gold enough, they take it and go their way; but if it does not seem to them sufficient, they go aboard ship once more, and wait patiently. Then the others approach and add to their gold, till the Carthaginians are content. Neither party deals unfairly by the other: for they themselves never touch the gold till it comes up to the worth of their goods, nor do the natives ever carry off the goods till the gold is taken away.

These be the Libyan tribes whereof I am able to give the names; and most of these cared little then, and indeed care little now, for the king of the Medes. One thing more also I can add concerning this region, namely, that, so far as our knowledge reaches, four nations, and no more, inhabit it; and two of these nations are indigenous, while two are not. The two indigenous are the Libyans and Ethiopians, who dwell respectively in the north and the south of Libya. The Phoenicians and the Greek are in-comers. It seems to me that Libya is not to compare for goodness of soil with either Asia or Europe, except the Cinyps region, which is named after the river that waters it. This piece of land is equal to any country in the world for cereal crops, and is in nothing like the rest of Libya. For the soil here is black, and springs of water abound; so that there is nothing to fear from drought; nor do heavy rains (and it rains in that part of Libya) do any harm when they soak the ground. The returns of the harvest come up to the measure which prevails in Babylonia. The soil is likewise good in the country of the Euesperites; for there the land brings forth in the best years a hundred-fold. But the Cinyps region yields three hundred-fold.

The country of the Cyrenaeans, which is the highest tract within the part of Libya inhabited by the wandering tribes, has three seasons that deserve remark. First the crops along the sea-coast begin to ripen, and are ready for the harvest and the vintage; after they have been gathered in, the crops of the middle tract above the coast region (the hill-country, as they call it) need harvesting; while about the time when this middle crop is housed, the fruits ripen and are fit for cutting in the highest tract of all. So that the produce of the first tract has been all eaten and drunk by the time that the last harvest comes in. And the harvest-time of the Cyrenaeans continues thus for eight full months. So much concerning these matters.

. They are useful, because they pick up all sorts of small animals and the offal thrown out of the butchers= and cooks= shops. They are troublesome because they devour everything, are dirty, and with difficulty prevented from polluting in every way what is clean and what is not given to them.

Vasco da Gama: *Round Africa to India*, 1497-1498 CE

1497 : The Bay of St. Helena [on the west coast of the present country of South Africa]. On Tuesday (November 7) we returned to the land, which we found to be low, with a broad bay opening into it. The captain-major [i.e., da Gama speaking in the third person] sent Pero d'Alenquer in a boat to take soundings and to search for good anchoring ground. The bay was found to be very clean, and to afford shelter against all winds except those from the N.W. It extended east and west, and we named it Santa Helena.

On Wednesday (November 8) we cast anchor in this bay, and we remained there eight days, cleaning the ships, mending the sails, and taking in wood. The river Samtiagua (S. Thiago) enters the bay four leagues to the S.E. of the anchorage. It comes from the interior (sertao), is about a stone's throw across at the mouth, and from two to three fathoms in depth at all states of the tide.

The inhabitants of this country are tawny-colored. Their food is confined to the flesh of seals, whales and gazelles, and the roots of herbs. They are dressed in skins, and wear sheaths over their virile members. They are armed with poles of olive wood to which a horn, browned in the fire, is attached. Their numerous dogs resemble those of Portugal, and bark like them. The birds of the country, likewise, are the same as in Portugal, and include cormorants, gulls, turtle doves, crested larks, and many others. The climate is healthy and temperate, and produces good herbage. On the day after we had cast anchor, that is to say on Thursday (November 9), we landed with the captain-major, and made captive one of the natives, who was small of stature like Sancho Mexia. This man had been gathering honey in the sandy waste, for in this country the bees deposit their honey at the foot of the mounds around the bushes. He was taken on board the captain-major's ship, and being placed at table he ate of all we ate. On the following day the captain-major had him well dressed and sent ashore.

On the following day (November 10) fourteen or fifteen natives came to where our ship lay. The captain-major landed and showed them a variety of merchandise, with the view of finding out whether such things were to be found in their country. This merchandise included cinnamon, cloves, seed-pearls, gold, and many other things, but it was evident that they had no knowledge whatever of such articles, and they were consequently given round bells and tin rings. This happened on Friday, and the like took place on Saturday.

On Sunday (November 12) about forty or fifty natives made their appearance, and having dined, we landed, and in exchange for the ‡eitils with which we came provided, we obtained shells, which they wore as ornaments in their ears, and which looked as if they had been plated, and foxtails attached to a handle, with which they fanned their faces. The captain-major also acquired for one ‡eitil one of the sheaths which they wore over their members, and this seemed to show that they valued copper very highly; indeed, they wore small beads of that metal in their ears.

On that day Fernao Velloso, who was with the captain-major, expressed a great desire to be permitted to accompany the natives to their houses, so that he might find out how they lived and what they ate. The captain-major yielded to his importunities, and allowed him to accompany them, and when we returned to the captain-major's vessel to sup, he went away with the negroes. Soon after they had left us they caught a seal, and when they came to the foot of a hill in a barren place they roasted it, and gave some of it to Fernao Velloso, as also some of the roots which they eat. After this meal they expressed a desire that he should not accompany them any further, but return to the vessels. When Fernao Velloso came abreast of the vessels he began to shout, the negroes keeping in the bush.

We were still at supper; but when his shouts were heard the captain-major rose at once, and so did we others, and we entered a sailing boat. The negroes then began running along the beach, and they came as quickly up with Fernao Velloso as we did, and when we endeavored to get him into the boat they threw their assegais, and wounded the captain-major and three or four others. All this happened because we looked upon these people as men of little spirit, quite incapable of violence, and had therefore landed without first arming ourselves. We then returned to the ships.

Rounding the Cape. At daybreak of Thursday the 16th of November, having careened our ships and taken in woods we set sail. At that time we did not know how far we might be abaft the Cape of Good Hope. Pero d'Alenquer thought the distance about thirty leagues, but he was not certain, for on his return voyage (when with B. Dias) he had left the Cape in the morning and had gone past this bay with the wind astern, whilst on the outward voyage he had kept at sea, and was therefore unable to identify the locality where we now were. We therefore stood out towards S.S.W., and late on Saturday (November 18) we beheld the Cape. On that same day we again stood out to sea, returning to the land in the course of the night. On Sunday morning, November 19, we once more made for the Cape, but were again unable to round it, for the wind blew from the S.S.W., whilst the Cape juts out towards S.W.. We then again stood out to sea, returning to the land on Monday night. At last, on Wednesday (November 22), at noon, having the wind astern, we succeeded in doubling the Cape, and then ran along the coast. To the south of this Cape of Good Hope, and close to it, a vast bay, six leagues broad at its mouth, enters about six leagues into the land.

When Did It Happen?

Match the date to the fact

1.   Song

A	B	C	D	E

2.   Shang

A	B	C	D	E

3.   Tang

A	B	C	D	E

4.   Zhou

A	B	C	D	E

5.   Han

A	B	C	D	E

1-5/ Choose the Correct Answer

a.   ca 1600-1000

b.   ca 1000-256 BC

c.   960-1276

d.   206 BC-AD 220

e.   618-906

---

6.   Children's Crusade.

A	B	C	D	E

7.   Genghis Khan invades China

A	B	C	D	E

8.   Fourth Crusade.

A	B	C	D	E

9.   Sixth Crusade.

A	B	C	D	E

10.   King John forced by barons to sign the Marna Carta

A	B	C	D	E

6-10/ Choose the Correct Answer

a.   1228

b.   1212

c.   1200–1204

d.   1211

e.   1215

When Did It Happen?

Match the date to the fact

11. Ming Dynasty begins in China.

| A | B | C | D | E |

12. The Great Schism (to 1417)

| A | B | C | D | E |

13. Mali Empire reaches its height in Africa under King Mansa Musa.

| A | B | C | D . | E |

14. Chaucer's *Canterbury Tales*.

| A | B | C | D | E |

15. Aztecs establish Tenochtitlán on site of modern Mexico City.

| A | B | C | D | E |

---

16. Ibn Battuta leaves on pilgrimage.

| A | B | C | D | E |

17. Invention of sawmill spurs shipbuilding.

| A | B | C | D | E |

18. Admiral Cheng Ho begins his voyages for Emperor Chu Ti.

| A | B | C | D | E |

19. Marco Polo journeys to China establishing the overland trade route.

| A | B | C | D | E |

20. Ibn Battuta returns home from his travels.

| A | B | C | D | E |

11-15/ Choose the Correct Answer

a.   c. 1325

b.   1368

c.   1378

d.   c. 1387

e.   1312–1337

16-20/ Choose the Correct Answer

a.   1271-95

b.   1325

c.   1328

d.   1355

e.   1405

When Did It Happen?

Match the date to the fact

21. Moors conquered in Spain by troops of Ferdinand and Isabella.

	A	B	C	D	E

22. Joan of Arc leads French against English

	A	B	C	D	E

23. Ivan the Great rules Russia until as first czar

	A	B	C	D	E

24. Incas rule in Peru.

	A	B	C	D	E

25. Turks conquer Constantinople

	A	B	C	D	E

---

26. Columbus makes landfall in the Bahamas on October 12

	A	B	C	D	E

27. Cortez enters, lays siege to, and conquers Aztec capital Tenochtitlan

	A	B	C	D	E

28. Ponce de Leon explores Florida on two expeditions

	A	B	C	D	E

29. Treaty of Tordesillas divides the New World between Spain and Portugal

	A	B	C	D	E

30. Pedro Alvares Cabral claims the Brazilian "hump" for Portugal

	A	B	C	D	E

21-25/ Choose the Correct Answer

a. 1492

b. 1438

c. 1462

d. 1453

e. 1428

26-30/ Choose the Correct Answer

a. 1492

b. 1494

c. 1513-21

d. 1519-22

e. 1500

Match the Terms

Instructions:
Place the number
next to the letter

Please match the terms below to questions 1-5.

a.   homo sapiens
b.   Neandertal
c.   Neolithic
d.   Australopithecus
e.   Homo erectus

---

1.   Hominid that lived from around 1.5 million to two hundred thousand years ago.

2.   Being capable of conscious thought.

3.   New stone age.

4.   This people thrived in Europe around one hundred thousand to thirty-five thousand years ago. They enacted deliberate burials complete with ritual observances.

5.   Order of primates that lived in Africa as early as four million years ago.

A. 2

B. 4

C. 3

D. 5

E. 1

Please match the terms below to questions 6-10.

a.   Hammurabi
b.   Moses
c.   Gilgamesh
d.   Yahweh
e.   Sargon of Akkad

---

6.   Known as the true founder of Hebrew monotheism.

7.   Hebrew god.

8.   He is known as the hero of the world's oldest known epic story.

9.   This powerful Babylonian king developed a sophisticated code of law.

10.   He was the first conqueror to unite Mesopotamia.

A. 9

B. 6

C. 8

D. 7

E. 10

Match the Terms

Instructions:
Place the number
next to the letter

Please match the terms below to questions 11-15.

a. Kush
b. Khufu
c. Osiris
d. Kashta
e. Hatshepsut

11. Largest of the pyramids.

12. Nubian kingdom.

13. She was the first woman to rule Egypt.

14. Later conquering Kushite king who ruled Egypt.

15. Egyptian god of the underworld.

Please match the terms below to questions 16-20.

a. Brahmins
b. Harappa
c. Indra
d. Karma
e. Samsara

16. The Aryan's chief god, associated with war and rain.

17. Priestly caste.

18. The reincarnation of the soul.

19. An early Indian city.

20. Hindu law of cause and effect.

A. 12

B. 11

C. 15

D. 14

E. 13

A. 17

B. 19

C. 16

D. 20

E. 18

Match the Terms

Instructions:
Place the number
next to the letter

Please match the terms below to questions 21-25.

a.   Mandate of heaven
b.   Book of Songs
c.   Shang
d.   Chu
e.   Zhou

21. Chinese dynasty (1766-1122 B.C.E.) dependant on the use of bronze technology.

22. Strong Chinese southern state.

23. This Chinese ideal asserted the leader's right to rule.

24. Collection of verses from the Zhou dynasty.

25. This dynasty (1122-256 B.C.E.) laid the groundwork for Chinese thought.

A. 2B

B. 24

C. 21

D. 22

E. 25

Please match the terms below to questions 26-30.

a.   Maya
b.   Olmecs
c.   Teotihuacan
d.   Pyramid of the Sun
e.   Mochica

26. This was the first Mesoamerican society.

27. This capable Mesoamerican society formulated writing and made great strides in mathematics.

28. This was both a Teotihuacan temple as well as the largest building in Mesoamerica.
29. This early Andean state left an extraordinary artistic legacy.
30. This post-Olmec state continued the development of the Olmec calendar and graphic symbols. It was known for its orange pottery.

A. 27

B. 26

C. 30

D. 28

E. 29

Match the Terms

Instructions:
Place the number
next to the letter

Please match the terms below to questions 31-35

a. Achaemenids
b. Marathon
c. Sasanids
d. Darius
e. Parthians

31. This Iranian empire's reign lasted from 247 B.C.E. to 224 C.E.

32. What did the Persians lose to the Greeks in 490 B.C.E.?

33. He was emperor of the Achaemenid empire during its highest point.

34. Cyrus founded this Persian empire.

35. This empire claimed direct descent from the Achaemenids and ruled 224-651 C.E.

Please match the terms below to questions 36-40.

a. Confucius
b. Mencius
c. Liu Bang
d. Qin Shihuangdi
e. Lao-tzu

36. Author of the Tao Te Ching and the founder of Daoism.

37. This post-Confucian scholar believed human nature is basically good.

38. This philosopher believed that social and political harmony arose from the proper ordering of human relationships.

39. This emperor unified China.

40. He was the most powerful emperor of the Han dynasty.

A.___

B.___

C.___

D.___

E.___

A.___

B.___

C.___

D.___

E.___

Match the Terms

Instructions:
Place the number
next to the letter

Please match the terms below to questions 41-45

a. Vardhamana Mahavira
b. Siddharta Gautama
c. Ramayana
d. Ashoka Maurya
e. Chandragupta Maurya

41. This leader was the first to unify India.

42. This Indian leader converted to Buddhism and became a dedicated missionary.

43. An Indian epic that chronicles the experiences of a hero and Sita, his wife.

44. A.K.A. the Buddha.

45. A highly respected Jainist scholar.

A.___

B.___

C.___

D.___

E.___

Please match the terms below to questions 46-50

a. Knossos
b. Pericles
c. Socrates
d. Salamis
e. Alexander

46. This philosopher propounded, "The unexamined life is not worth living."

47. Persia was conquered by which Macedonian leader?

48. A pivotal naval battle in the Persian War.

49. This was the center of Minoan society.

50. Athens became the Cultural center of the Greek world due to which leader?

A.___

B.___

C.___

D.___

E.___

Match the Terms

Instructions:
Place the number
next to the letter

Please match the terms below to questions 51-55.

a. Patricians
b. Tiberius Gracchus
c. Paul of Tarsus
d. Etruscans
e. Augustus Caesar

51. Who spearheaded the expansion of Christianity beyond Judaism?

52. The reunification of the Roman world and the *pax romana* are due to what leader?

53. Ancient Roman wealthy class.

54. Rome's early history was dominated by which Northern Italian tribe?

55. His campaign for land reform led to his murder.

A.___

B.___

C.___

D.___

E.___

Please match the terms below to questions 56-60.

a. Alaric
b. Constantine
c. Diocletian
d. Chang'an
e. Zhang Qian

56. He divided the Roman empire into eastern and western halves.

57. He established an eastern capital for the Roman empire.

58. Rome was sacked in 410 C.E. by which Visigoth ruler?

59. This Chinese messenger's travels aided in the establishment of the silk roads.

60. The eastern end of the silk roads.

A.___

B.___

C.___

D.___

E.___

Match the Terms

Instructions:
Place the number
next to the letter

Please match the terms below to questions 61-65.

a. Justinian
b. Belisarius
c. Leo III
d. Theodora
e. Prince Vladimir

61. He initiated iconoclasm.

62. Justinian's wife.

63. This Byzanitne emperor tried to restore Rome's earlier glory.

64. Byzantinian general who won southern Spain, northwestern Africa, Sicily and Italy.

65. He assisted in the conversion of Russia to Orthodox Christianity.

A.___

B.___

C.___

D.___

E.___

Please match the terms below to questions 66-70.

a. Quran
b. Abu al-Abbas
c. Abbasid
d. Hajj
e. Sharia

66. Islamic holy book.

67. Islamic legal code

68. One of the five pillars of Islam.

69. He founded the Abbasid dynasty.

70. This ruling dynasty was centered around Baghdad.

A.___

B.___

C.___

D.___

E.___

Match the Terms

Instructions:
Place the number
next to the letter

Please match the terms below to questions 71-75.

a.   Zhu Xi
b.   Samurai
c.   Tang Taizong
d.   Murasaki Shikibu
e.   Huang Chao

71.   He stole from the rich and gave to the poor.

72.   Neo-Confucian scholar.

73.   He wrote *The Tale of Genji*.

74.   Strongest Tang emperor.

75.   Professional Japanese soldiers.

A.___

B.___

C.___

D.___

E.___

Please match the terms below to questions 76-80.

a.   Delhi sultans
b.   Harsha
c.   Ramanuja
d.   Bhakti
e.   Mahmud of Ghazni

76.   This movement tried to dispel the distinction between Islam and Hinduism.

77.   This devotee of Vishnu pressed for a more personal connection to the diety.

78.   In the 11th century, he led several pillaging expeditions into India.

79.   They ruled northern India from the 12th to the early 16th centuries.

80.   Seventh century Buddhist emperor/scholar who rejoined northern India.

A.___

B.___

C.___

D.___

E.___

Match the Terms

Instructions:
Place the number
next to the letter

Please match the terms below to questions 81-85.

a. Charlemagne
b. Clovis
c. Alfred
d. Leo III
e. Serf

---

81. Strongest Carolingian ruler.

82. This West Saxon king bested the Danes and helped to unify England.

83. Leader of the Franks and convert to Christianity.

84. Which pope gave an imperial crown to Charlemagne?

85. Unfree peasant.

A.___

B.___

C.___

D.___

E.___

Please match the terms below to questions 86-90

a. Mehmed II
b. Golden Horde
c. Genghis Khan
d. Mahmud of Ghazni
e. Khubilai Khan

---

86. Ottoman Turk who captured Constantinople.

87. Mongolian leader who pillaged Persia and conquered northern China.

88. Mongol tribe that dominated Russia.

89. This 11th century Turkish leader pillaged India.

90. Mongol ruler who supported culture and Buddhism.

A.___

B.___

C.___

D.___

E.___

Match the Terms

Instructions:
Place the number
next to the letter

Please match the terms below to questions 91-95.

a. Mansa Musa
b. Sundiata
c. Axum
d. Ghana
e. Mali

91. Ethiopian Christian kingdom.

92. Strongest Mali ruler who made a pilgrimage to Mecca in 1324.

93. The kingdom of Mali's legendary founder.

94. Powerful west African state that first developed in the 5th or 6th century C.E.

95. Between the 13th and 15th centuries, this African kingdom dominated trade across the Sahara.

A.___

B.___

C.___

D.___

E.___

Please match the terms below to questions 96-100.

a. Hugh Capet
b. Gregory VII
c. William of Normandy
d. Urban II
e. Franciscians

96. In 1066 England was conquered by what leader?

97. This pope excommunicated Henry IV as part of the investiture conflict.

98. Anti-materialistic religious order that forbade personal posessions.

99. Pope responsible for promoting the First Crusade.

100. He was elected French king in 987.

A.___

B.___

C.___

D.___

E.___

Match the Terms

Please match the terms below to questions 101-105.

a. Tula
b. Pachacuti
c. Tenochtitlan
d. Huitzilopochtli
e. Motecuzoma II

101. Aztec empire's last ruler.

102. Aztec chief god.

103. Inca leader who started the expansion of the empire.

104. Capital city of the Aztec empire.

105. Chief Toltec city.

A.___

B.___

C.___

D.___

E.___

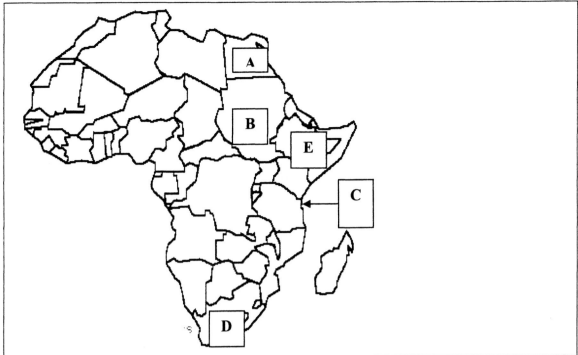

Instructions:
Choose the letter which identifies the
location for each subject.

1.   Zanj City-states

| A | B | C | D | E |

2.   Great Zimbabwe

| A | B | C | D | E |

3.   Memphis was its capitol

| A | B | C | D | E |

4.   Axum

| A | B | C | D | E |

5.   Kush

| A | B | C | D | E |

6.   The San people

| A | B | C | D | E |

7.   Meroe

| A | B | C | D | E |

8.   Swahili

| A | B | C | D | E |

9.   Alexandria

| A | B | C | D | E |

10.   Massai

| A | B | C | D | E |

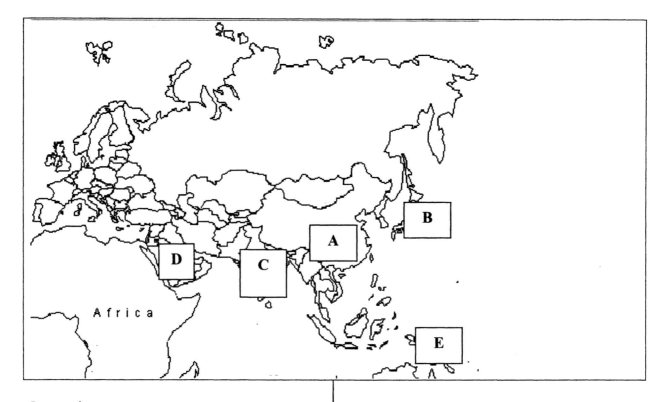

Instructions:
Choose the letter which identifies the
location for each subject.

----

1.   Indus Civilization

A   B   C   D   E

2.   'Yangshan'

A   B   C   D   E

3.   Legendary Emperor Jinmu

A   B   C   D   E

4.   Hinduism originated here

A   B   C   D   E

5.   6,800 islands

A   B   C   D   E

6.   Sanhuangwudi may be myth

A   B   C   D   E

7.   First Civilizations

A   B   C   D   E

8.   Silk Road

A   B   C   D   E

9.   First rice growers

A   B   C   D   E

10.   Sumer

A   B   C   D   E

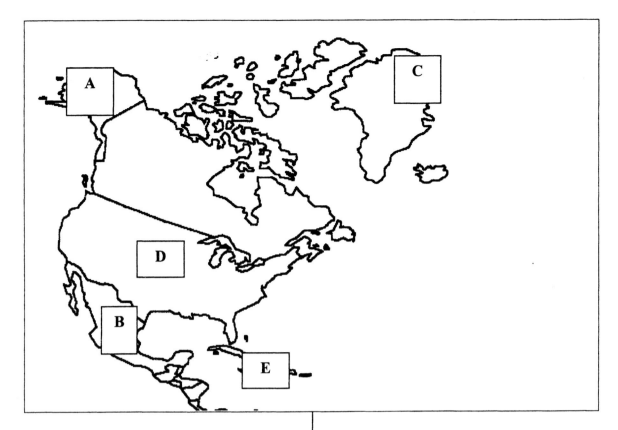

Instructions:
Choose the letter which identifies the location for each subject.

----

1.   The Bering Straits

| A | B | C | D | E |

6.   Named after an Italian

| A | B | C | D | E |

2.   Early Viking Settlement

| A | B | C | D | E |

7.   Inuit people

| A | B | C | D | E |

3.   Olmecs

| A | B | C | D | E |

8.   Cherokee Nation

| A | B | C | D | E |

4.   Columbus first arrived here

| A | B | C | D | E |

9.   Primary food is Maize

| A | B | C | D | E |

5.   John Cabot explored

| A | B | C | D | E |

10.   Mayans

| A | B | C | D | E |

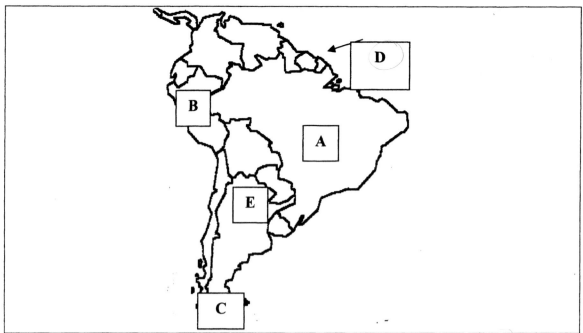

Instructions:
Choose the letter which identifies the
location for each subject.

----

1.   Tierra del Fuego

A	B	C	D	E

2.   Incas

A	B	C	D	E

3.   Cabral

A	B	C	D	E

4.   Chavins

A	B	C	D	E

5.   Strait of Magellan

A	B	C	D	E

6.   A British colony in this region

A	B	C	D	E

7.   Also a Dutch colony is here

A	B	C	D	E

8.   Amazon Basin

A	B	C	D	E

9.   Solis visited in 1516

A	B	C	D	E

10.   The Diaquita

A	B	C	D	E

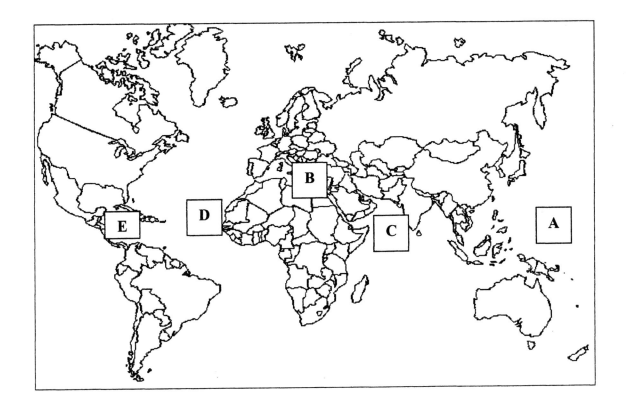

Instructions:
Choose the letter which identifies the location for each subject.

----

1.   Youngest of world's oceans

A	B	C	D	E

6.   Greek for 'Sea of Atlas'

A	B	C	D	E

2.   Romans called it their 'Lake'

A	B	C	D	E

7.   Zambezi River flows into it

A	B	C	D	E

3.   Named by Magellan

A	B	C	D	E

8.   Second only to Pacific in size

A	B	C	D	E

4.   Mare Nostrum

A	B	C	D	E

9.   The West Indies

A	B	C	D	E

5.   Third Largest body of water

A	B	C	D	E

10.   'Arawaks' lived here

A	B	C	D	E